STILL BLACK, STILL STRONG

STILL BLACK, STILL STRONG

SURVIVORS OF THE U.S. WAR AGAINST BLACK REVOLUTIONARIES

DHORUBA BIN WAHAD
MUMIA ABU-JAMAL
ASSATA SHAKUR

Edited by Jim Fletcher, Tanaquil Jones, & Sylvère Lotringer

SEMIOTEXT(E)

Semiotext(e) Offices:
522 Philosophy Hall, Columbia University, New York, NY 10027
POB 568 Williamsburgh Station, Brooklyn, NY 11211

(718) 387-6471

Printed in the United States of America.

Contents

Dhoruba Bin Wahad

... Ahmad Abdur-Rahman (released)

Mumia Abu-Jamal (death row)

Sundiata Acoli

Alberta Wicker Africa (released)

Carlos Perez Africa

Charles Sims Africa

Consuella Dotson Africa

Debbi Sims Africa

Delbert Orr Africa

Edward Goodman Africa

Janet Holloway Africa

Janine Phillips Africa

Merle Austin Africa

Michael Davis Africa

Ramona Johnson Africa (released)

Sue Leon Africa (released)

William Phillips Africa

William Allen ...

War Within
Prison Interview

Dhoruba Bin Wahad: My name is Dhoruba Al Mujahid Bin Wahad. Formerly Dhoruba Moore. I'm a political prisoner. I've been incarcerated in New York State for nearly nineteen years, which I guess makes me one of the longest held political prisoners in the world, a notoriety I do not seek, but there it is. My imprisonment was a result of my activities in the Black community as a member and leader of the Black Panther Party. My case has been recently argued in an appellate court in New York State after a judge ruled on a motion filed by myself that evidence was withheld in my case that would have overturned my conviction on direct appeal. And because the government withheld its evidence for eighteen years, my direct appeal has been exhausted. So essentially I remain in prison on a legal technicality. That's the legal status

*This interview was conducted by Chris Bratton and Annie Goldson in the fall of 1989 at Eastern Prison in Napanoch, New York, approximately seven months before Dhoruba Bin Wahad was released on his own recognizance after his conviction was vacated. The interview also appears in Bratton and Goldson's documentary film, **Framing the Panthers**.*

of my case. Right now there are over a hundred political prisoners and prisoners of war incarcerated in the United States and serving exceptionally long sentences, and most of them are Black militants and former members of the Black Panther Party. My case has received a considerable amount of notoriety in that I was one of the original defendants in the New York Panther 21 conspiracy case which involved an indictment against the leadership of the New York Chapter of the Black Panther Party in April of 1969.

Q: And you were part of that original indictment?

DBW: Yes. At that particular time the Black Panther Party was under full-force attack from the United States government, which subsequently destroyed the Black Panther Party. I used to travel around the country speaking about that case and other political cases so I always had to go through a lot of changes with the FBI at the airports, State Troopers pulling us over on the highway, the whole nine yards. It became really crazy. I felt I was in a war. I would walk down a street and if kids threw firecrackers, man, I would duck. The only reason we wouldn't shoot back was that we had a policy to see who it was first. It stayed that way until I was arrested. You could see by some of the photos how I looked. I looked like one of those POW's in the early stages of the battle outside Laos—you know, Vietnam. I was completely shell-shocked. I had a combat mentality. It was a question of survival. It was them or me. I was targeted as a "Black extremist" and put into the United States government's "Agitator Index" and "Black Extremists" files. These files were meant to identify and target certain leaders and spokespersons of the Black struggle for human rights so that they could be neutralized and otherwise taken out of circulation.

Q: The sentence you're serving now, was that on charges unrelated to the 21 trial?

DBW: It's unrelated to the 21 case but it's a continuation of the political repression that was aimed at myself and at the Black Panther Party at that time. You see, when I was acquitted in absentia in the 21 case I was a fugitive, forced underground by the FBI's Counterintelligence Program (COINTELPRO). COINTELPRO had devised a plot to incite the national leadership of the Black Panther Party to assassinate me and some of my comrades.

Q: How did you become aware of that?

DBW: During my civil suit against the government, around 1980, I eventually got them to release a bunch of documents under the heading "Travel of BPP National Leadership." And one of these documents indicated that there was, in fact, a counterintelligence program aimed at creating a split between the New York Black Panther Party and the BPP National Headquarters. The FBI wanted to sow suspicion in the minds of national leadership, specifically Huey P. Newton, David Hilliard and the Central Committee in Oakland, California, that the New York Black Panther Party members were out to kill them. They would go about this very systematically. They would send letters to Huey P. Newton purporting to come from New York Panthers who were disgruntled because they didn't adhere to the instructions of the Central Committee. They would also capitalize on individual differences, on the sexism and on the regionalism within the Black Panther Party. You should remember that the BPP was a national organization, and when you travel across the country you see that each city has a different rhythm, and style. The FBI would try to use these differences to divide the Black Panther Party. One operation specifically mentioned that I was opposed to representatives of the Central Committee who were stationed in New York to administer the everyday affairs of the Black Panther Party after the Panther 21 arrests. The Panther 21 were the leadership of the NY Chapter of the Black Panther Party, and for a number of years they were in prison, so the office of the Black Panther Party sent cadres and other field workers to New York to help run the party. So when I was released on bail the FBI started a program to sow dissension between myself and the individuals who were left in prison and between myself and the individuals who were put in leadership positions from the West Coast. And this resulted in my being demoted in rank, this resulted in friction between myself and the leadership which was already under stress, and culminated in threats on my life during the time of the Panther 21 trial. It was a result of these threats on my life that I had to flee underground, during a crucial point in my trial, and the government tried to portray my disappearance as an admission of guilt. Of course it was all designed to prejudice the jury because the evidence in the case was very weak. I imagine the State thought that if the Panthers who were on bail fled right before the deliberation, that would sort of sway the jury into believing that they were guilty. But that had nothing to do with it. We had to jump bail because the Counterintelligence Program had devised a plot to kill us. Of course we became very paranoid. I felt that I was always under pressure. Since the BPP leadership had chosen me to be released on $100,000 bail, I felt the Black Panther Party had a $100,000 investment in me. I couldn't sleep in the same place two nights in a row. I always had to have people on security with me.

Q: What happened then?

DBW: While I was a fugitive, two New York City police officers were shot and wounded as they were guarding the home of Manhattan District Attorney Frank Hogan. The following day two New York City Police officers were shot and killed in Harlem. Now both of these shootings were claimed by the Black Liberation Army—

Q: Which was a clandestine group.

DBW: Yes. According to the United States Senate Church Committee on terrorism in the United States, the Black Liberation Army grew out of the Black Panther Party. The way it's portrayed in official documents is that the Black Liberation Army represented the hardcore militants within the Black Panther Party who were dissatisfied with legitimate struggle, with legitimate protests. Of course that's not true. The racist repression of the Black Panther Party is what motivated the Black Liberation Army. The destruction of the Black Panther Party, the splitting of the Black Panther Party into hostile factions, is what led to that particular development of the Black underground in the United States. These activists, who could no longer function safely above ground, had to flee for their survival. So I was a fugitive. I was underground when these two officers were shot on May 19, 1971, and the BLA claimed responsibility for these shootings. At that time the Black community was enraged by the continual murder of Black youth by the police and the ongoing racist police brutality that was being inflicted on the Black community. The Black underground retaliated in this way. I wasn't involved in any of these shootings, but because of my notoriety around the Panther 21 case, because of my vocal opposition to the criminal justice system in New York, I became a prime target for a frame-up around the shooting of these two officers. I maintained then and I maintain now that I was innocent of that shooting.

And subsequently, as a result of my filing a suit in the Federal District Court in Manhattan, I obtained approximately 300,000 pages of FBI documents on the Black Panther Party, on myself, and on the Counterintelligence Program, and these documents clearly indicate that: (1) I was a target of the Counterintelligence Program of the United States government and the New York law enforcement agencies; and, (2) I was innocent of the charges for the murder of these two officers. When we first got these documents they were heavily excised. I filed this suit against the U.S. government in 1975 and it took over five years for me to prove that the government was lying about its COINTELPRO role in my case.

Q: And how did you first learn of it?

DBW: It was in the newspapers, the Church Committee hearings on FBI misconduct.

Q: And then you suspected that you—

DBW: Well, knowing that I was innocent of the charges and that I was a target of the United States Government, I immediately contacted some attorneys that I knew and requested that they file a civil suit charging civil rights violations and demanding that all of the counterintelligence documents in my case be turned over to me. And we went through a long litigation process. This was in 1975. At first the United States government and the police denied any involvement in any such counterintelligence activities. They did this for several months. They tried to overturn the civil complaint on purely technical grounds. We survived that. And, for almost five years, they stonewalled it. It so happened that at that particular time a suit was being litigated in Chicago in the case of Fred Hampton.

Q: And what was the Fred Hampton suit?

DBW: As you recall, Fred Hampton and Mark Clark were leaders in the Chicago Chapter of the Black Panther Party who were assassinated on December 4th, 1969, by the local Chicago police. Their murder was set up by an FBI informant who had infiltrated the BPP and rose through the ranks of the Chicago Chapter to become its Security Chief. He supplied the Chicago Police Department with a layout of the apartment. And it was that agent that drugged Fred Hampton into unconsciousness. Fred Hampton was murdered in his sleep, in bed next to his pregnant fiancée, by the Chicago Police Department. At first it was reported that it was a shoot-out between the Black Panthers and the police, and the police were just defending themselves. But subsequently it was found out there was only one shot fired by the Black Panther Party members who were in the house. Scores of other shots were fired into the house by the police, murdering and maiming the occupants. So Fred Hampton's murder became the clearest example of the escalation in the repression of the Black Panther Party.

Up until this particular time the Panthers were always portrayed by the mainstream media as gun-toting criminals, urban terrorists, violence-prone Black men and women. And the police were always portrayed as the innocent victims of Panther attacks and hatred. But the Fred Hampton case clearly showed that there was a conspiracy to murder Black Panthers and destroy the organization.

Years later a suit was filed against the Chicago Police Department by the family of Fred Hampton and it was during the litigation of that suit that certain documents came to light. Some of these documents had my name on them and they were not among the documents that were turned over to me during my suit. So when this was brought to the attention of the federal judge, she got a little upset and ordered the U.S. government to turn over everything with my name on it. And this flood of documents began coming in. And it should be noted, too, that around this same time the New York City Police Department claimed it had lost its intelligence files on the Black Panther Party. They claimed this for almost ten years. Then we started producing certain documents from the FBI that indicated that the source for the FBI was the intelligence unit of the New York City Police Department.

Q: Have you received any of those NYPD documents?

DBW: We received about three hundred irrelevant documents— surveillance of demonstrations. They said they lost the whole file. Well they found the file about three years ago sitting in a room in One Police Plaza. Nobody knew it was there, see. They miraculously found this whole room stacked from floor to ceiling with documents. Their next legal maneuver was to claim that the newly found documents were privileged material, so we had to fight a motion in court for privilege. It's these types of dilatory tactics that in any other case would not have been tolerated by the court.

Q: Why were they tolerated in your case?

DBW: Because it clearly showed that the law enforcement agencies of the United States government and the state of New York had broken the law in order to put me away. And because of the political nature of the case, because of the police officers that were shot, the lives of those police officers that were involved, the credibility and the political interests of the Policemen's Benevolent Association (PBA), and other agencies, it required that the courts bend over backwards in order to give them the opportunity either to destroy the evidence, doctor evidence, or conceal it, and that's what the court did. And it still does that today. To this very day the suit is pending. It's been pending since 1975. It's one of the longest pending suits in the Seventh District Court. What are we talking about here? Fourteen years or something? Not bad for an old suit.

Q: Could you describe what COINTELPRO was, and give some indications of its breadth?

DBW: In the Church Committee report, there's a glossary of terms. And in this glossary are the different acronyms and accepted terminology that are used in the intelligence community. And "counterintelligence" usually and universally means to counteract the intelligence operations of a foreign power. However, COINTELPRO, as implemented by the FBI, was aimed at countering the rise in political power of a domestic national minority— specifically, primarily, Black people. But when it was first devised, as we well know, it was aimed at the Communist Party, USA. That's when it was first devised, in terms of the acronym—COINTELPRO, counterintelligence program. I think that's very insightful, because the FBI had no charter to deal with foreign intelligence operations outside of the United States, only domestically. And the CIA, which came along after World War II, had no charter to deal with domestic surveillance, only with foreign intelligence matters outside of the United States. And if you have viewed any old newsclips of J. Edgar Hoover, who was the long-time director of the FBI during the fifties, during the so-called Civil Rights Movement, you will see that on a number of occasions, when asked whether the FBI would protect civil rights workers in the South who were being attacked by racists, murdered by Klansmen, Hoover made it a point of stating that the FBI had no police functions, that it was merely an investigative arm of the U.S. government. The implementation of the Counterintelligence Program transcended mere investigation. It was in effect a domestic war program, a program aimed at countering the rise of Black militancy, Black independent political thought, and at repressing the freedoms of Black people in the United States. The Counterintelligence Program can be seen as a program of war waged by a government against a people, against its own citizens. It was a program of domestic warfare.

It could be compared, in some respects, to the counterintelligence activities that were carried out in Southeast Asia, around the time of the Vietnam War. I have specifically in mind operations carried out in Laos, the secret war in Laos that was carried out by the CIA. Of course the analogy has its limitations. The military in Laos, for instance, were able to carry out larger operations. There was a counterinsurgency program secretly financed by the U.S. government through the CIA that destroyed whole villages in regions of Laos. We could say that this was not the case in the United States, but it was just a matter of scale here, and proportion. In the United States, the equivalent of the military was the local police. During the early sixties, at the height of the Civil Rights

Movement, and the human rights movement, the police in the United States became increasingly militarized. They began to train out of military bases in the United States. The Law Enforcement Assistance Act (LEAA) supplied local police with military technology, everything from assault rifles to army personnel carriers. So, the Counterintelligence Program went hand-in-hand with the militarization of the police in the Black community, with the militarization of the police in America. I think that this was a crucial turning point in the development of the modern nation-state. The so-called "intelligence community" developed and honed its skills at domestic repression under the guise of local law enforcement and the Counterintelligence Program.

Q: What do you think were the ideological and political justifications that they were hoping to present to the public?

DBW: One of the things that motivated the militarization of the police in the United States was racism. They really believed that Black people and national minorities, people of color, American Indians, Puerto Ricans and Chicanos, represented a serious threat to the internal security of the United States. And I think that that was based on the historical fact that these national minorities had been subjugated by a racist system for centuries, and that if they were to exercise the full panoply of political, economic and social rights, the American system as such, in its Eurocentric character, could no longer carry out its mission. The mission of the American nation-state is to perpetuate European hegemony over the Third World and over people of color. Political education and the development of political awareness was one of the main goals of the Black Panther Party. In fact the BPP never posed a serious military threat to the U.S. Government. It was the popularity of our 10 Point Program, our belief in the guaranteed right of everyone to food, clothing, decent housing, free health care, education, etcetera, that terrified the government and motivated them to launch an all-out attack against us.

Q: But one of the immediate ways of doing that was to criminalize, as you say, independent-thinking people of color, to present them as criminals.

DBW: Well, yes, that has always been a unique characteristic of political repression in the United States, going back to slavery. When we look at the history of the development of slave laws, in the ante-bellum South, we see that there was a whole legal system put into place to keep the African enslaved. Anyone that rebelled against this legal system was in effect a criminal. They were subject to be prosecuted by the courts. The slave codes were, in effect, penal codes in many parts of the country. And it's not a coincidence that today the United States denies that it has any political prisoners, based on the fact that everybody in prison is convicted of a crime. I mean, we didn't just pop out of the ground this morning. Everything has a history. And it's no coincidence that the prosecutorial agencies of the State make no distinction between political repression and law enforcement.

Q: What have been the long-range effects of COINTEL-PRO on the Black community?

DBW: The most devastating effect of the Counterintelligence Program in the Black community in America has been the vacuum of leadership that it created. Now, this vacuum was filled in the seventies by individuals who survived the repression of the sixties because they were not involved in front-line struggles. And the ones who had been involved in these struggles were thoroughly intimidated by the awesome devastation of the Counterintelligence Program. I think the deaths of Malcolm X and Martin Luther King and the destruction of certain militant organizations created a vacuum in the Black community, and this vacuum was filled in many cases by political charlatans, opportunists and individuals who were less than uncompromising in their stand against race repression and racist domination.

Q: So you're suggesting that King and Malcolm X were probably targets of COINTELPRO?

DBW: Well, I have no doubt that they were. I think that the events surrounding the deaths of both Malcolm X and Dr. Martin Luther King indicate that the U.S. government had a hand in manipulating forces to murder them. If we go back historically into the demise of all potent revolutionary Black leaders we'll see that almost in every instance other Black people were used to murder them, or to compromise their struggle.

Q: What about COINTELPRO's effects internationally?

DBW: The purpose of the Counterintelligence Program on the international level was the isolation of Blacks from the international community. And it was this purpose that I believe was at the root of the deaths of both Malcolm X and Dr. Martin Luther King, because both of these Black leaders had begun to speak about international issues and attract an international audience. The majority of the so-called Black leaders who do enjoy a degree of international credibility are those who usually collaborate with U.S. foreign policy interests. So, the Counterintelligence Program, in my view, had an international component, and its operations on the international level were carried out by the CIA. The CIA had a program similar in form and objective to COINTELPRO called "Operation Chaos." It dealt with domestic surveillance and international surveillance of domestic activists, and to this very day no one knows the depths of that program.

But I think the objective of the Counterintelligence Program on the international level was the isolation of the Blacks from the events of the Third World, and that this isolation was a very important aspect of U.S. foreign policy. It has been consistent U.S. government policy, regardless of whether the administration has been Republican or Democrat. In its attempt to portray itself as a bastion of freedom, of free speech, of human rights, the U.S. has consistently had to overcome the racist origins of its own foreign policy and its own interests. American foreign policy and interests are Eurocentric. Yet the majority of the nations of the world are people of color. So the COINTELPRO operations that were aimed at muting the voice of Blacks in the international arena were a very important component in maintaining U.S. supremacy over the Third World. We need to examine that, and we need to examine how it is that we have come into the position where sports figures and entertainers can travel abroad and act as spokespersons for Black people, act as our representatives abroad. This is a sad state of affairs and Black people need to put this dynamic in check. I think the best way to do that is to send a signal to Black athletes, to Black actors, to Black musicians, that they are just actors, athletes and musicians. They do not speak for Black people on the international or social or political level. I think this would help us, to a great extent, to remove the myth that Black Americans are satisfied with the American Dream, and instead transmit to the world that we are living the American nightmare. We need to separate ourselves from the image of America abroad and establish our own identity as a people and represent that identity to the world at large.

Q: The FBI sought to present the Black Panthers and other militants as criminals, but actually one of the results of the repression was that it did force people to use arms in an offensive instead of defensive manner. Do you see that as one of the effects of COINTELPRO?

DBW: When we talk about methods of resistance, we need to understand a basic principle. And that basic principle is that repression breeds resistance. And the more vicious and physical the repression, the more intense and physical the resistance. A lot of people do not understand that the Black Liberation Army, as an idea and as a concept, was a response to the brutal repression of the Black Panther Party, and the legalization of that repression. Even though the FBI and other government agencies wiretapped the phones and homes of activists within the Black Panther Party and other organizations, these wiretaps, by and large, were illegal. They were not supported by existing law. They were wiretaps that were authorized by the Attorney General, John Mitchell, solely under his authority. So here you have an agency that purportedly is committed to defending the law and defending the U.S. Constitution, breaking the law and bending the law in order to repress elements in society that it views with disfavor. That that has been typical of law enforcement agencies. The state, the national security state—which America is—has one overriding interest, and that is to protect and defend itself against its own citizens. Anything that the police did, anything that the investigative agencies of the government did in order to defend the national security state interests, was considered legal, was considered "justifiable." Now the fact that subsequent to the deaths, murders, exiles, and imprisonment of scores of political activists, a U.S. Congressional committee says that these methods were reprehensible, is beside the point. I mean, it's like saying today that chattel slavery was an inhumane system. OK, it's an inhumane system, but what do we do about it, what have we done about it? Do we change history? Have we taken actions to rectify that in our culture, in our way of thinking, in the passage of laws? No. To this very day the police carry out illegal surveillances, they manipulate and utilize the law to repress the individuals that the government has problems with, and that's the reality. And the American public is conned into believing that they're just doing their job, and they're just defending society from violence-prone individuals.

Q: Why do you think you in particular, and the Black Panther Party generally, became such an obsession for the U.S. government?

DBW: I think it was psycho-sexual... I say that only partly tongue-in-cheek. One of the things that scares white America is the thought of assertive Black manhood. They cannot deal with the threat that it represents to white male supremacy. And some of that is psycho-sexual. The idea of Black men standing up in America in a para-military array, so to speak, with guns— it scares the hell out of white folks. It was the idea that had to be destroyed. The individuals may not have represented a significant physical threat to the United States government, it was the idea that Black men had the right to defend themselves against white aggression. That's psycho-sexual. Women tend not to be perceived as as great a threat, and often for this reason when they become revolutionaries they break the sexist mold. Historically, Black women were always at the forefront of the struggle. Certainly Harriet Tubman, Sojourner Truth and Assata Shakur, among others, inspired fear in the white man's heart. During slavery, men and women were forced to work side by side in the field. They were whipped and tortured with equal vehemence. The psycho-sexual component of our oppression was evident in the extent to which violence against us took on a sexual flavor. White males have always been allowed unhindered access to Black women. In fact, rape was an essential feature of the chattel slave system, used to dominate, humiliate and control Black women. Lynchings invariably involved the dismemberment of sexual organs (breasts, penises, testicles). These acts were condoned because Black men and women were typically viewed as animals or chattel, subhumans. So when you stand up in the twentieth century with a gun in your hand, and you're not presenting a middle class amenable to the "reason" of white standards and white values, then you become a threat. But the power of that threat didn't just come from nowhere... I'm not saying that the only underlying motivation for our oppression is psycho-sexual, that would be overly simplistic. But this is what lurks behind the notion of Black people armed for their own defense— fear of Black potency. The idea of Black self-defense couldn't be tolerated.

Q: Some psycho-sexual elements are evident even today?

DBW: Yes, and they have to do with Black assertiveness. America gets very belligerent with its prerogatives if its rights are trampled on by other people, especially Third World people or people of color. And the first thing they want to do is send in the Marines. They get real macho. They talk about the right to self-defense, the right to be armed, you know, the armed citizenry. But there is definitely a dual standard here. White male supremacy is a given. Black subordination is also supposedly a given, and the Black Panther Party changed that. It's no coincidence that law enforcement agencies, staffed mainly by white macho males, just went berserk at the mere thought of Black people, mostly Black men, shooting back at them. I mean, they went crazy. The fear of Black men and Black males is so pervasive in this society that a mob in Bensonhurst or a mob in Howard Beach could murder men just based on the fact that they're in the neighborhood, or that they look at you in a certain way, or that they wear their hat a certain way, or that they carry themselves a certain way, with aggressiveness. I found this same fear throughout my time in prison, that it's very difficult to deal with prison officials unless they feel that you are being subservient. And me, being the type of individual that I am, I don't feel or act like I'm subservient. I recognize that I'm in prison but that's as far as it goes. I mean, it's not my prison. If it was my prison I wouldn't be here, right? There's a basic assumption that as a Black you are expected to communicate in your demeanor and in the tone of your voice that you believe you are inferior and they are superior. And when you refuse to do that, you have a problem. And if you have no power, you become the victim of the problem. My point was that the Black Panther Party had to be destroyed because of the idea that it represented, Black assertiveness and Black self-defense, that this should be achieved by any means necessary, in fact by the same means, if necessary, that white people would employ to defend themselves. And the system couldn't tolerate that.

Q: What about the political dimension of the Black Panther Party? Did that represent a threat as well?

DBW: I think the idea of the Black Panther Party was one catalyst behind Lyndon Baines Johnson's launching his Great Society Program. Black people have never really progressed unless there was that tension and dynamic between advocates for a radical change and those who advocated reform. As long as there wasn't a Malcolm X to play to a Martin Luther King or a Whitney Young, the system would ignore the entire question.

Q: Why did you choose the Black Panther Party?

DBW: My background indicated to me that things wouldn't change and folks wouldn't respect or even deal with us if we didn't stand up and defend ourselves against racist attack. I mean, would the United States have withdrawn from Vietnam if it wasn't for the NLA, if it wasn't for the struggle of the Vietnamese people to determine their own destiny? Would the French have withdrawn from Indochina if it wasn't for Dien Bien Phu? Would they have withdrawn from Algeria if it wasn't for the FLN?

Q: Do you see a similarity between colonized people in the Third World and the situation of Blacks in the United States?

DBW: Yes, there are similarities but there are also significant differences. I don't think colonized people who have been the victims of European colonialism and imperialism over the last two centuries really understand the nature of the European nation-state, and the mentality that's behind it. They believe that they could take their place in the world community of nations behind these European models. History has shown that that won't work. They have deluded themselves. They have bought into some of the incarcerated ideologies that are at the basis of the European nation-state. Blacks in the U.S. are different in this respect. We've lived so close to European Americans, we have had such an intimate relationship with them over such a long period of time, that we really understand what they're about. We have no illusions about what they're about. I mean, even your basic unemployed laborer in Harlem understands what white folks are about. He may not be able to articulate it as well as Jesse Jackson, or as some other "Black leaders," but he understands at a deep psychological and gut level. And I don't think that Third World people who have not lived with white Americans, with Europeans, understand that.

Q: What are white people about, and how does that affect the nation-state?

DBW: When I use the term "white people" I'm talking about a certain cultural/historical continuum, as opposed to individuals. Because, as you know, individuals are capable of transcending certain sociological and ideological limitations. But at the same time we're all soldiers of history, I guess, we're all in the same stream of history. So when I say white people, I'm talking about a social, economic, and historical confluence of forces that determines the social being and consciousness of large segments of people and informs their relationships with each other. That's basically what I mean when I say that. The European historical experience is the experience of self-alienation. And the reinforcement of that experience through the political and economic establishment of the

28

modern nation-state has led to the present situation that we're in. If we check out any aspect of Europe's involvement in the world, we'll see that alienation and greed have been the primary motive forces in everything they do. That alienation has manifested itself in their encounters with aboriginal cultures. Just my limited reading of Europe's colonization and appropriation of the North American continent shows me that they had a certain mind-set that came from the European historical experience. The fundamental contradiction of that mind-set is the human alienation from self and nature, a seeing, a perceiving of oneself as being over and above nature. It's a unique feature of European culture. I mean, no other people have that, not to that degree. Eastern cultures are more holistic, more unified in their approach to life, and in their approach to the struggles of life. But it's that contradiction, inherent and inculcated in the European historical experience, that has transformed the nature of the world. If you look at the destruction of the environment, it goes right back to that. I mean, how could you dump toxic wastes in the environment and think it's not going to have an effect on you, unless you think you're above nature? So unless you think along the line of unity with the universe, of being connected, a part of rather than apart from nature, you can't begin to build the type of moral government that could heal the planet, that could do away with genocide and war, exploitation, or hierarchies of domination and brutal control.

Q: When you were in the Black Panther Party, what sort of work were you doing?

DBW: I used to organize chapters and branches of the Black Panther Party throughout the state of New York and along the Eastern Seaboard, down to Maryland. We started out working with tenants in Harlem, organizing tenant strikes, getting involved in squatting struggles. People didn't really know that abandoned city buildings could be taken over, that they could go to court and get the property just by developing it and living on it. We got involved with students on the various campuses around New York City — college and high school students — around the issues of Black studies. Also with the development of drug-free rehabilitation centers, where the therapy involved the consciousness-raising of the drug addicts, and getting them off drugs. One of the major struggles at the time was around the Lincoln Detox (detoxification) center in the South Bronx. It was called "Think Lincoln." The city administration intended to make it a methadone program, and we had taken it over along with the Young Lords Party. The Young Lords Party was an organization of Puerto Rican youth and students that was modelled along the lines of the Black Panther Party. We had a good working relationship with the Young Lords Party in East Harlem, and with the Young Patriots Party, which was an organization of white students and youth from lower Manhattan. In effect it was this relationship that developed into what became the earliest Rainbow Coalition. So you see Jesse Jackson's concept of the Rainbow Coalition came from the Black Panther Party, which most people don't know, and I'm quite sure Jesse would 'fess up to it, if he was asked. I mean, after all, our brother Jesse is an honorable man. But the type of work we did was community work, working with tenants, working with welfare mothers, students. We began to develop programs for community control of the police, in fact we were struggling to petition to get on the ballot for 1969 the question of the decentralization of the New York City Police Department.

That particular issue grew out of the attack on Panthers at the courthouse in Brooklyn by off-duty police officers. Three Panthers were arrested in a demonstration in Brooklyn and charged with illegal use of a bull-horn, things of that nature. They were beaten by the police and taken to the Brooklyn court for an arraignment. The Black Panther Party had mobilized hundreds of supporters to go down to the courthouse when they came up for a hearing. At that time in Brooklyn there was a fascist police organization called LEG — the Law Enforcement Group. It was headed by various elements in the police department who felt the PBA was too soft. They were at the courthouse in force too, along with hundreds of policemen, and they attacked the Panthers and the civilian demonstrators. The police that were on duty gave them the nightsticks and they beat us in the courtroom and out on the street. A number of Panthers were sent to the hospital and arrested and Mayor Lindsay vowed to look into this because he was told off-duty officers had broken the law, etc. We filed a suit in court and demanded that the New York City Police Department be decentralized. We presented a whole program, we floated the idea of community control. We had hit upon the concept of a community control board, which would review compulsive police brutality. It would be staffed by individuals who were not police officers. And the PBA mounted a big campaign to confuse the issue in the newspapers, in the media, on the subways, and throughout the city, saying that if you were for the community review board, vote no, and if you were against it, vote yes. And it worked! I mean, everybody that was for it voted no, and everybody that was against it voted yes. So, it was voted down. It sounds crazy, but it happened. If you would review some of the clippings of the period you'll see it, right there.

The type of work we did at that time revolved around trying to better the conditions of Black people in the inner city, in housing, in school, in welfare, in hospital care. We opened free hospital clinics so that people could be tested for sickle-cell; we secured volunteer doctors from different hospitals around the city; we opened free breakfast programs to feed children during the school months. That's the type of activity that we engaged in. And, of course, we also organized self-defense patrols in the Black community. We advocated that Black people arm themselves against racist attack. That seems to be the part of our agenda that got the most attention.

Q: I wanted to read you a selection from the Panther 21 statement delivered to Judge Murtow: "Does not your constitution guarantee man's freedom, his human dignity against state encroachment, or does the innate fear of the rebellious slave in the heart of the slave master continue to this day to negate all those guarantees in the cases of Black people?"

DBW: We had divided up the writing up of that statement and I wrote that part. The key phrase in there is the innate fear in the slave master for the slave, for his rebelliousness. The so-called "rebellious slave" was the one that was always singled out for a special type of treatment, as an example and a signal to the rest of the slaves that—this is what will happen to you if you rebel against our power and against our system. And often the rebellious slave, the strong Black slave, would be subject to heinous physical torture. He—or she, would have the skin flayed off his or her back, would be hung in a tobacco shed, to twist and twist for days until he died, or he would have a bit put into his mouth like a horse. And he'd be branded and put into shackles and irons: he would have his limbs chopped off so he couldn't run anymore; he would be castrated, or, in the case of the rebellious female slave, raped, then lynched, burned. And all of these things always ended up or began with the destruction of the genitals. Again, it's all psycho-sexual. When we deal with how the criminal justice system in America reacts to the idea of a Black person actually breaking the law that penetrates and circumscribes their condition of servitude and oppression, the system will stop at nothing, including its own law, to destroy that. And it means one of two things: either that Blacks are not human, or considered human, by the state and therefore their rights and their lives and property are not held sacred by the Constitution; or there is a dual standard of justice in which the constitutional rights of the majority culture are incapable of working for the minority culture, in which case we have come to the final question in my view, which is the tyranny of majority rule in a racist culture. The modern nation-state that we know as America was not founded on a principle or idea of absolute equality under the law, even man-made law. It was founded on the principle that those who are born into property and privilege are somehow "more equal" than everyone else.

As a Black, when I go into the courtroom, can I expect equal treatment under the law? What's done and just for white people or for European males in American society is not going to be equal to what's done to me in a racially supremacist society. I read somewhere that the educational system in America is designed to teach Europeans about themselves. The Constitution works—for white folks! They don't have no problem with it. I got a problem with it. Because all men are not created equal. And this society has perpetrated that fraud on Black people so that they would continue to labor in the vineyards of the American Dream without seeing any results, and there's nothing that can be done about that within the context of this nation-state. The nation-state is a European concept which is blocking the development of humanity.

Q: You've talked about the European desire to dominate, in psycho-sexual terms, and also in terms of historical and cultural superiority. You haven't really mentioned the sort of acquisitive side of European culture which—

DBW: That development has always manifested itself in early mercantilism, in the so-called era of exploration and discovery. I mean, the place didn't exist until the Europeans discovered it. They discovered China, and all of the millions of people that were living there and dying there for the last five thousand years didn't know they were there. They became actors on the world stage only when they encountered Europeans. The Euro-centric view of history, as we know it, it's in anthropology, it's in everything. Do you know how long the anthropologists argued that the origins of humankind couldn't be in Africa? It wasn't until just recently that the *New York Times* finally 'fessed up and said, "All the genes in the human pool can be traced back to our aboriginal ancestor in East Africa." Do you think that would have been the case in the 1800s, when they were propounding all these theories of a "white man's burden"? Give me a break! The evidence was there, the information was there. I read somewhere that "the age is not dark because people are ignorant, but because people refuse to see." The Dark Ages of Europe was a period in which the Europeans couldn't see. So how does this relate to us today, in purely economical terms?

The purpose of the modern European nation-state was to accumulate capital. To accumulate wealth. That's what it is, that was its complete reason for existence. And in doing that, it appropriated other people's land, other people's wealth, and other people's rights. The formation of the whole nation-state concept is relatively new. I mean, it coincided with the development of capital, it coincided with the disintegration of the feudal system in Europe, and it led to a period of unprecedented expansion and imperialism. This is how that inferiority manifests itself economically. Europe had the audacity to sit down in the late 1800s and divvy up Africa. I mean, just divvy it up! Like there were no people there. And then when they realized, seventy or eighty years later, that they had to get out of Africa, that they had relied upon the mineral resources and wealth and exploitation of those resources for their own development, they came up with a new idea, the idea of the Commonwealth of Nations, organizing the whole region so that indigenous African governments would find it impossible to develop their own economies without cooperation with these European nations. So artificial boundaries were set, and people were, willy-nilly, given independence, and you might have one nation that's completely land-locked, with no means to export its resources, and another nation that has all these ports, but no resources to export. One speaks French and the other speaks English, so the French and the English mediate the whole thing, you see? We'll get your goods out for you; we'll build a railroad for you; we'll send your children to the Sorbonne, and educate them, and we'll put these elites back in there so they can rule over your own people. So we have the development of neo-colonialism. Neo-colonialism is the last stage of imperialism. I mean, there is an economic basis for it all.

There are probably valid reasons for it, but the only ones that deal with it are Black scholars. We delve into it because we need to understand why all these people treat us the way they do. We have to find out, we have to know why. But the

35

people that treat us this way don't want to find out, and they don't want to know why. I guess it's because it makes them feel kind of guilty. A well-meaning individual who might not harbor any overt racist animosities, basically a decent guy, or a decent woman, will say, you know, I resent it when you say I am responsible for this. I wasn't there three hundred years ago, I didn't have slaves. It's the standard argument, right? I didn't do it. I'm innocent. But that's not the point. The point is that he inherited white-skin privilege, and he hasn't questioned or challenged it. I mean this is something I'd really like people to deal with, even our Black leaders don't put this question to society. We have to talk about Mayor Koch, one of the most reactionary mayors New York has had in a long time, an individual who has been totally insensitive to the historical condition of Black people in the city under his administration. And this individual begins to talk about binding the wounds of racism, building monuments to racial harmony in New York. Why do we always have to talk about reconciliation, healing wounds of a racial division when Black people die, but when white people die they talk about revenge, they talk about justice, about putting someone away for life?

There's no reconciliation there. Why? Because the value of a Black life and the value of a white life are different. It's completely obvious, and no one questions that. And the politicians, the white politicians that stand up and say that's not true, and if I became mayor I would punish these men to the fullest extent of the law, etcetera, they're hypocrites. You only hear them when one of us gets killed. Because they fear the attitude of Black people should change from trying to fit into the American dream of white folks to destroying it. That's the fear. So it's only the reconciliation when we die. It's justice when they die. You see? People try to make a comparative analysis between the rape of a white woman in

Central Park by Black youth with the murder of Yusef Hawkins by a white youth. They say, no one demonstrated in Harlem when this woman was raped. I'm not trying to diminish the horror and terror of rape, that's not my point. My point is to say that one is a crime, and the other one is a crime because of race, it is based in a racist historical continuum. The question has to be asked whether the same outrage would have been exhibited if it was a Black woman who had been raped in Central Park by white boys. Would it? There's never been a white man sent to the electric chair in American history for raping a Black woman. Never. Check the books. Never. So if I was to hold a white man, or white male society responsible for the rape of a Black woman, then I would be an extremist, you see? If I was to value Black womanhood to the same degree as white males claim to value white womanhood and virtue, I would be considered a Black nationalist extremist. That's what J. Edgar Hoover said we were, Black nationalist extremists, and that justified what he did to us, in his eyes, and in the eyes of the U.S. government.

Q: Could you outline the nature of the repression that the United States visited on the Black Panther Party?

DBW: Well, I think that it was essentially a continuum of the repression that they visited on all movements for Black liberation since we've been in this country. I mean, the Garvey movement was destroyed by essentially the same tactics that were utilized against the Black Panther Party. His organization was infiltrated, his reputation was denigrated, he was boycotted economically by certain elements in the Black community who were being manipulated by the government, and by white economic interests in the Black community, and he was eventually destroyed as an effective Black leader of

37

Black people because of what he advocated. The same was true of the Nation of Islam and Malcolm X. The Nation of Islam was infiltrated by agents of the U.S. government, and this is an organization that was essentially apolitical and pro-capitalist, albeit Black capitalist. The Nation of Islam was never a revolutionary political organization but it represented a threat to the U.S. government because it was disciplined. It was an organization that had a certain cohesive, ethical, and moral basis for its discipline, and it followed a particular leader. One of the objectives of the initial memo regarding the Counterintelligence Program vis-à-vis the Black movement was to prevent the rise of a Messianic leader who could unite Black people. You have to understand that the individuals who run and control the system, have the entire apparatus of academia at their disposal. Some of the best minds of the world can be found in the institutions of higher learning in the United States. And these individuals are paid and contracted by the U.S. government to analyze how we think, how we feel, to analyze every facet of our existence, to conduct experiments on us emotionally, psychologically, and physically. This has been done. So the Counterintelligence Program, when it was implemented against Black people, was a war strategy that fed on the weaknesses of Blacks.

There was nothing haphazard or incidental about COIN-TELPRO. In the documents, former F.B.I. director J. Edgar Hoover talks about the standards of moral conduct that hold sway in the African-American community. And, being a racist, he says that these standards are essentially low-life standards, they're different from white standards, so you really can't embarrass these negroes by calling them names and showing that they're corrupt in certain ways, because they're not like us, you see? That's what they did to the Vietnamese people. Look at Professor Pike's study on the Vietcong. He analyzed the Vietcong from the village level, from the family level, all the way up to the highest bureaucrat in the NLF. The Phoenix Program was designed to take advantage of this type of analysis. It murdered and killed thousands of Vietnamese people.

And a lot of these tactics were brought home to the United States and employed in the Black community. A lot of police officers got their initial training in counterinsurgency and counterintelligence in Vietnam. Some police officers went on sabbaticals to serve in the Phoenix Program during the Vietnam War. Concepts like block watches, and community patrols, and community outreach programs, were all further developments of the ideas and concepts that were outlined to destroy the Vietcong—the village watcher, the spy who could inform the police as to who was an NLF cadre and who wasn't. These techniques, the techniques of disinformation, of counterinsurgency—they were brought home. The war was brought home to the United States. When we used to say that the war was being fought in our community at home, the peace movement, which was predominantly white, predominantly liberal, ignored us. They didn't want to confront and deal with their racism. It was all right to talk about "Stop the war in Vietnam," because that threatened their future. They could be the ones to be drafted. But they didn't want to deal with the war in Watts, with the war in Buttermilk Bottom in Atlanta, with the war on Hastings Street in Detroit. They didn't want to deal with that because that was too close to home. And even today we see that in the anti-interventionist movement in Central America, organizations that are involved in supporting the Nicaraguan struggle are not as vocal in supporting the struggle of Black people. They're not even involved in it. It repeats itself. Again, we go back to the original premise of self-alienation in European history. If you're not dealing with you roots, and where you're coming from, then it manifests itself in how you approach contemporary politics.

Q: Do you think the white American Left stood by as the Black Panther Party was destroyed?

DBW: Yes, I think so. The Black Panther Party absorbed the rage and the repression that would have normally been visited on the white Left. I mean, every time I read one of these "Sixties Revisited" interviews or books where they will go to a sixties radical and they will ask: "What was it like?" and the white radical might be sitting up in a yuppie bar, and, you know, he's a corporate executive, and he says: "Well, it was wild, man..."

Meanwhile you have Blacks who are in the grave, who are in prison, who are in exile, and they don't have that privilege of reflecting. Essentially white America said to their children: "Alright, you sowed your wild oats, you did your thing, now come into the system." White privilege was always there for them to come back to; it was never there for Black people. The system was taking no prisoners, no hostages, when it came to repressing us. But when it came to repressing their own children, the really crazy ones, the ones who meant what they said and were really out there, they dealt with them, like Marilyn Buck or the Ohio Seven. But then again, the class basis of the Ohio Seven is completely different; they come from working-class families, they're poor.

Q: Could you tell us more about the sorts of strategies the FBI used against the Black Panther Party?

DBW: Well, there were a number of strategies. It depended on what they wanted to achieve. Their primary goal was of course to achieve the total discreditation of the Black Panther Party. If they could have discredited the Black Panther Party in the eyes of Black people without putting everybody in jail, I'm reasonably certain that they would have done it. There is one document, a memo from the San Francisco FBI field office to Bureau headquarters, which says that the underlying purpose of the Counterintelligence Program is to bring home to Black youth that if they adhere to, or succumb to, the revolutionary philosophies or ideologies, they will be dead revolutionaries. The document says—I'm still paraphrasing—that Black youth need something to believe in, and we have to prove and show to them that it's better to be accepted by the system than to tear it down. They wanted to prevent the passing on of ideas that the Panthers represented to Black youth. And they were successful at that. In my mind this was the most painful document to read because of the condition that Black youth are in today. They have no understanding of history, of their past. They have become, to a large extent, very nihilistic. They have succumbed to the base materialism and materialistic attitudes of American society. I mean, look at the gangs in L.A., and the gangs in Chicago, and in New York City. Black youth are cut off from any sense of purpose or direction, from any sense of social responsibility and political struggle. That was the reason the Black Panther Party had to be destroyed.

One of the first objectives was to "prevent the rise of a Mau-Mau rebellion in the U.S." COINTELPRO utilized all types of tactics. One tactic was identifying effective leaders within the Black Panther Party, and then creating rumors around these particular individuals so that the leadership would feel threatened, and therefore neutralize them. Another tactic was to develop contradictions within the party over money. In one memo, J. Edgar Hoover says that the three things a "Negro" wants most are money, a white woman, and a Cadillac. (Laughs.) That's the way he said it, you know. (Laughs again.) Homeboy was a funny dude. Some of it was just funny. I mean, I remember reading one report, in a SWAT team training manual, where they were thinking of using red smoke and red dye in the suppression of urban violence because they said that red really messed Black people up. A lot of the programs sound ludicrous when you read them on paper, but they employed them, and they worked. I mean, they worked, man.

Q: In terms of creating divisions—

DBW: Yeah, in terms of creating division, confusion. You have to understand, too, that the U.S. government had strong media contacts in all the major networks throughout the country, so they would leak a story to the press saying that, for instance, Huey P. Newton's position was being threatened, and the media would lead a story—"Panther Rivalry Feared." It's the same with Bush, today, with his "Here I have a vial of crack that was purchased right across the street from the White House"—that old tired routine. He had the DEA (Drug Enforcement Agency) go find somebody who sold drugs, brought him across the street from the White House, purchased the drugs, and then he gets on television with this serious look, you know, we are on the front lines of this war, right at my gates they are selling this stuff! And I'm the president, so I know how you feel, fellow Americans, and we're going to get these guys. That was perfect. Every network played it. Over and over again. Until some bureaucrat

DEA agent who's probably now pounding a beat in Chittlin' Switch, Georgia, somewhere, came out and said, "Well, you know, we did that, had to B.S. for the White House."

So it's the same thing—the government creates the scenario, the law enforcement agencies present it to the media, and the media gobbles it up and presents it as a fact. I mean, the analogies abound. That's the same thing as the old law-and-order ruse from the sixties. When the ghettos were going up in flames, when Black people were marching in the streets, when fists were being thrust in the air, demanding Black Power, the term law-and-order meant "keep the niggers in their place." That's basically what the term meant. And they would present images of these enraged Black youth on the screens that scared white America to death. They would show a phalanx of Black Panthers, everybody looking serious and appropriately gruesome, and wearing black, and black berets, and scare white folks to death.

Don't they do the same thing when it comes to Iran? Don't they show a million pictures of black-clad Iranian women chanting, "Death to America!" And then they flash to an airliner that was blown up in mid-air, and then they speculate that it might be a retaliation by the Iranians for the shooting down of the air-bus. This sends a certain message to people, and the message is that those Iranians are blood-thirsty fanatics who hate Americans, so anything you do to them is justified. Therefore when Iranians are murdered, as in the air-bus incident, no one deals with their humanity. The first thing they have to do in order to repress a people is to denigrate their humanity, reduce them to something less than human, make them into a threatening Other, and then you can do anything you want to them. You can lock them up and put them in prison, like they did me, you can murder them, like they did Fred Hampton and Mark Clark, or Twyan Myers, or Zayd

Malik Shakur, or you could exile them, like they did Michael Tabor or Assata Shakur. That's what the system does. It first strips you of your humanity, reduces you to the level of a mad dog, and a depraved terrorist, and then it's open season, they can do anything they want to you.

That was one aspect. Another aspect was to disrupt the Black Panther Party's ability to disseminate its ideas. The second most important program, in my view, from analyzing the documents that the U.S. government had, was to destroy and disrupt the circulation of the Black Panther newspaper. That was number two on their agenda, behind destroying the credibility and legitimacy of the Black Panthers. The Black Panther paper at one time had a circulation of three-quarters of a million copies a week. It was not only a source of considerable revenue for the Black Panther Party, because the paper sold at twenty-five cents apiece, but it was also a means by which the Black Panther Party got its ideas across to Black people. So they devised a counterintelligence program to capitalize on cartoons. Now, you look at cartoons, and you see them as harmless. But that is the incorrect conclusion. A picture is worth a thousand words. During World War II the art of the poster and of the cartoon to portray the enemy as someone that was heinous and someone you should just march off to, willingly lay your life down to kill, became a high art form. So what the U.S. government did...

VOICE: The officer at the desk will now be accepting money for empty accounts...

DBW: What COINTELPRO did, they manufactured a coloring book, and in the book they put various anti-Semitic slogans and pictures. They circulated the coloring book, and they said that this was the book that was being given out to

44

children at the Free Breakfast Program. And there was a big Senate investigation on this. It was designed to show that the Black Panthers were anti-Jewish. And of course, the Black Panther Party wasn't anti-Jewish; the Black Panther Party, in its ideologies and its perceptions, was anti-Zionist. Now, while it may be true that all Zionists are Jews, it doesn't necessarily mean that all Jews are Zionists. Zionism is a form of reactionary nationalism, as it is manifested in the European settler-state we know as Israel today. So the Black Panther Party, on a principled level, opposed Zionism. That was distorted to upset the alliance between liberal Jews and Blacks, especially liberal Jews who supported the state of Israel.

They used other devices. They had a "Dear Irving" letter. The FBI would write this letter to prominent Jewish figures, or organizations. And this Irving character would purportedly be a disgruntled communist. And he would say how he was privy to information that the Black Panthers were anti-Semitic, they were talking about killing all the Jews. And this would, of course, get all these philanthropic Jewish organizations and leaders all uptight. They would demand an investigation of the Black Panther Party, and they would come down on any liberal Jew who supported the Black Panthers. A good example was the Leonard Bernstein affair. As you recall, Leonard Bernstein, a well-known conductor, and a liberal Jew in New York, gave a cocktail party to support the Panther 21, who were in prison. He invited his friends to come and hear what the Panthers had to say. And the Panthers came. They spoke, and they solicited funds towards the bail of the Black Panther Party, and this idiot—Wolfe—what was his first name? Tom?

Q: The one who wrote—

DBW: Yeah, *Radical Chic*. And he called it: "Hob-nob-bing with the Mau-Mau's," something like that. And he was very successful, I mean, the media took off, it was a great book, the whole nine yards, right? The FBI took the incident, and they wrote "Dear Irving" letters to different liberal organizations to isolate Leonard Bernstein. They brought a lot of pressure on him and his wife, and he eventually backed up from supporting the Black Panther Party. Subsequently, when the documents were released in my case, he was appalled and shocked by the fact that all of the letters he thought were legitimate were in fact from the FBI. Well, of course, he's never done anything since. Hey, I mean, it's water under the bridge. Those are just examples of how the government would utilize its access to the media. They did the same thing with a church group in New York that was considering bailing out the Panther Party. They notified their archdiocese that this particular church was holding meetings trying to raise money for the Panthers who were in jail for alleged acts of terrorism. And the archdiocese went off— they leaked the story, so the press came out, "Church Group Considers Bail for Jailed Panthers." This scared the preacher and he withdrew his support.

Q: Was there a difference in strategies between the local and the national?

DBW: Yes, there was. The national government has access to a greater amount of information, and greater resources, therefore its tactics could be more subtle and have a greater impact. Also they served as a clearing house which passed on certain information to the local police, which enabled them, of course, to manipulate the local police to do certain things, as in the murder of Fred Hampton and Mark Clark.

VOICE: The officer will be accepting change…

DBW: The Chicago police became the physical instrument by which a local Panther leader was assassinated and removed from the scene. And the FBI stood behind the scenes, manipulating the whole thing. The same's true in New York. The various District Attorneys brought the indictments against the local leadership of the Black Panther Party, prosecuted them, and put them in prison on state charges. Subsequently, in my case, for instance, once the conspiracy charges didn't stick and proved to be one of the greatest political embarrassments to the Manhattan District Attorney's office that they had had up to that point, then the local police, and the local prosecutor, went in to bring straight criminal charges in order to convince the jury that the issue at hand had nothing to do with politics. These cops were shot, and although we don't have enough direct evidence that this individual did it, we have circumstantial evidence and this is enough for conviction. Of course the jury, not knowing about the existence of COINTELPRO, didn't realize that the circumstantial evidence, to a significant degree, was fabricated, so they took it at face value, and I was convicted after three trials. The difference between the national and the local police then is that the local police served as the more direct physical instrument of eradicating and neutralizing the local Black Panthers, whereas the FBI dealt with the BPP on a national level and the Black struggle as a whole. So I guess you could say one was more a manipulative factor, and the other a direct repressive factor.

Q: Just hold on a sec. Let's change the tape.

DBW: They close the visiting room at 3:30.

Q: Yeah. We've got about half an hour. The final question I want to ask you is, picking up on what you said earlier about counterinsurgency in Vietnam and counterintelligence here at home, in the United States, do you see a relationship between those two and the subsequent development of counter-terrorism?

DBW: Sure. Once the Counterintelligence Program had been successful in destroying the ability of the Black Panther Party to work overtly in the Black community, and splitting its leadership, forcing certain individuals underground, then it changed its gears into a counterinsurgency or anti-urban guerilla program. In fact, the document names changed. It changed from COINTELPRO, or Black Nationalist Hate Groups, to Urban Guerrilla Black Nationalist Hate Groups. So the strategies changed. In fact, in 1971 the FBI convened a series of seminars in which it brought together police chiefs from all different parts of the country, and of various intelligence units, and gave them seminars on the threats of urban terrorism and the threat of the Black underground, the BLA, the FALN, the Weather Underground, and various other organizations that were considered terrorists in the United States. As a result of this, certain programs came into being. One program was called Prison Activist Program. In this program, correction officers from all over the country were brought together at the Marine Base in Quantico for workshops, and they were shown how they could play a crucial role in monitoring the activities of political prisoners, their visitors, and individuals in the street. Each facility had an officer that was identified as the individual who would be the liaison with the FBI. So that, like in my case, if the officers shook down my cell and found some "subversive literature," they would take the literature from my cell, and that literature would wind up in the hands of the FBI. Mine was the first case in which the New York City Police, New York State Police, and the FBI joined forces to conduct an investigation into the shooting of police officers. This was formalized later into what we now know as the Joint Terrorist Task Force. My case was the pilot project for that, as one of the memoranda of a police inspector indicated.

And the tactics that were used to disrupt the overt organizations became purely military tactics. That's when you see the development of SWAT teams in the United States. They first came as a result of the clashes between the Black Panther Party and the police throughout the country, when the police would raid Black Panther offices. The Black Panther offices tended to be fortified and heavily armed because we actually believed in self-defense. Therefore when they would attack the office, they would have APC's— armored personnel carriers— and helicopters. So they started to develop their special weapons and armed tactics. SWAT team tactics. And these SWAT team tactics were basically BUT tactics, Basic Unit Tactics, utilizing advanced weaponry training that you find in the military, adapted to the urban situation. A lot of the experienced personnel in these situations were Vietnam vets. In New York, it's the same thing with the Emergency Service Unit. So, yes, there is a direct correlation between the anti-insurgency that the United States fought abroad and the repression of the Black movement in the United States. By way of another example, we can see that the development of special forces, of quick emergency response teams, have coincided with the development of these units on the local—

police—and national level. Every police department that's worth its salary has a SWAT team, a special weapons and tactics squad. Every one. I mean, it goes with the territory now. These tactics are designed to deal with the rising tide of militancy, or contain that discontent.

Another example is this so-called war on drugs. Drugs were always used in the Third World as a mechanism of economic and political control. The classic example is China and the Opium Wars, the introduction of opium into China in order to facilitate European exploitation and dominance. So the military is being touted, and recruited, to fight the war on drugs, at least at the borders. The whole idea of a war on drugs is a domestic war policy. It's a code word for "keep the Black and Latino and surplus labor and youth in their place." And what's their place? Prison. Build more prisons. You can't employ them, you can't educate them, because the economy can't provide jobs for them. I mean, this is clear. So how do you deal with this? You declare a war on drugs, and you build armies, based on waging this war on drugs. In L.A. where we have these nihilistic gangs, youth gangs, going around, shooting each other with MAC 10's and AK 47's the people are screamin' and hollerin', "we need more cops!" And more cops you'll get. You'll see them on the Geraldo Rivera show kicking in doors, and how do they look? They look just like a SWAT team going into a village in Vietnam. That's what they look like! The only thing, they didn't land in a helicopter. They come in a van, they jump out, and they're armed to the teeth.

Sure. I mean, we should understand *glasnost*. The nature of *glasnost* is that the Europeans who control the Soviet Empire and those who control the European Empire realize that they have a common historical root. Now they have a common destiny: to maintain their control over the Third

World. The contradiction is no longer East–West, it's
North–South. So, that being the case, there has to be some
type of ideological basis for unity. It's no longer cool to say
the communists are the enemy; now they're coming over,
they're hanging out. Before you know it, you'll have joint
maneuvers between the Soviet Navy and the U.S. Navy. Who
are they maneuvering for, if they aren't fighting each other
anymore? We're talking about nuclear disarmament, so we're
talking about building a conventional arsenal. Who are the
major suppliers to the arsenals of the Third World? The same
parties that are talking about *glasnost*. So "anti-terrorism"
substitutes itself for "anti-communism." Anti-terrorism substitutes itself for blatant racism. It's no longer chic to say that
you should hang Black folks by a tree and lynch them, so
what you do is you declare them terrorists and you shoot 'em
in the head. That's the significance, in a nutshell, of how terrorism is replacing certain catch-words in the United States.

It's very important to understand that historically the
Third World has only been offered two paths to the development of their people, two methods of struggling—one was the
capitalist path, the so-called bourgeois democratic method,
and the other one was the so-called socialist or communist
method, the war of national liberation. Islam offers the third
one that both scares the Westerners to death and helped com-
pel *glasnost*. Today, one of the catchwords that goes with terrorism is what? Muslim fundamentalism. You ask the average
white American what is a Muslim and they'll tell you a
Muslim's an Arab. What is an Arab? An Arab is a terrorist.
He doesn't realize that Arabs are a minority in Islam. In fact,
only one-fifth of all Muslims are Arab. The majority of
Muslims happen to be, by the way, Indonesian. And Asian.
African. There are more Asian and Indonesian Muslims than
there are any other type. Islam, in the personification of Iran,

presented for the first time a path to liberation that before had never been opened to Third World people. You have to understand that there are almost a billion, nine hundred something million Muslims in the world who speak five hundred languages, and they're all united around one ideology and one primary source of faith. So the Iranian revolution represents a significant divergence from the East-West contradiction. The Iranians, through use of Islam, through their faith, and the methodolgy of Islam, overthrew a tiger—the major European powers and the United States. They didn't have guns, but they overthrew it overnight. That fundamentalism has been on the rise for the last twenty years throughout Africa, throughout the Middle East. The Intifada is essentially an Islamic uprising. The PLO is only incidental to that, which is one of the reasons Arafat, and the PLO, are anxious to negotiate a settlement. Because the Intifada was controlled by Muslims. We see the establishment of Islamic states throughout Africa, the Middle East, as an increasingly popular objective and goal. This threat of fundamental Islam, what's called fundamentalism, in essence is a methodology of liberation and struggle, based on a concept of the oneness of creation. It represents something the West or East cannot deal with. First of all you had the atheistic culture of the Bolsheviks, and they couldn't deal with it; and the materialistic, amoral culture of the West definitely can't deal with it. Then you have the historical contradiction between Islam and Europe, because for 700 years Muslims dominated a third of Europe.

Terrorism is being used because the conflict is no longer intended to be East vs. West. That no longer satisfies the industry of the Russians or of the United States, but they have a common basis: they are racists in Moscow, and they are racists in Washington, and they both have the same European historical root. They have to continue to control the European empires, be it the empire in Asia—which is called the Soviet Socialist Republic—or be it the empire in the Third World—Latin America or Africa. In order to fight that war, they have to fight terrorism. So you can believe that the first joint maneuvers between the U.S. military and the Russian military will be anti-terrorist maneuvers, and designed militarily and logistically to fight Third World Struggles that are fundamentalist in nature. I think that tells us a lot. I just wanted to indicate that any analysis of terrorism today would be incomplete if it didn't recognize that Glasnost and Detente, and the coming together of the East and West on economic and political issues, international issues, is directly related to nine hundred million Muslims... You gonna edit that stuff out?

Q: We've got about ten minutes. Recently, it seems, there was a court decision that came down in your favor. Could you talk about what that finding actually means, and what will happen to you?

DBW: Well, the recent decision by the New York State Supreme Court basically said that the prosecutor in this case, who is a federal judge now, had withheld massive amounts of evidence from me, evidence that was exculpatory. Now the judge, however, had ruled that, because of a leading case in his particular department, he could not overturn my conviction because that case had stated that there was a different criterion for the evidence. So we're waiting to see if this judge will do what the law requires him to do. You should keep in mind that in all political cases in the United States, the government and the courts have collaborated to deny the application of the law to political prisoners. Very seldom is law impartially applied to rectify the oppression of the State.

Q: So what do you speculate will happen?

DBW: Well, I speculate that the Court will be forced to overturn my conviction.

Q: And that means you'd be out of prison.

DBW: Yeah.

Q: How do you feel about that prospect? I mean, is it hard to handle?

DBW: No, it's not hard to handle being out of prison. It's hard to handle being *in* prison. I watched Nelson Mandela on television when he was released and when he stepped out of the prison hand-in-hand with Winnie Mandela, and I sort of felt, or imagined that I felt, some of the things that must have been going through his mind, and how he was feeling. And it's not easy to reconcile the fact that you've spent most of your adult life in prison because of certain political positions you've taken against your people's oppressors. In a lot of respects it would have been better if you were killed during the course of the struggle rather than buried alive in prison. And it's very difficult also to realize that in America, because they do not recognize the existence, or they do not own up to the existence of political prisoners, you are forced to live your life in prison by these two standards—by a very subtle standard of criminalization on the one hand, and a political, special treatment on the other. And the special treatment is not favorable, it's always to you detriment. For instance, you are never treated the same as everyone else, but then again, you're not the same as everyone else, you're not a social criminal in that sense. So it's very difficult, because the

Department of Corrections and other agencies of the State have a vested interest in breaking you spiritually and morally, of convincing you that you're nothing but a common criminal. And then when we deal with that in the context of the American situation, where the movement for Black liberation was so effectively repressed, and destroyed, and fragmented, that political prisoners in America do not enjoy the same mass-based principled support that political prisoners in other countries enjoy—again, South Africa comes to mind. The South African experience has shown that the ANC and the other anti-apartheid organizations have always made the freedom of political prisoners an integral part of their everyday struggle, of their demands for an end to the apartheid system. Now in America, that's not the case. In the United States we have Black leaders, Black elected officials, and some of the more prominent ones come to mind—David Dinkins, the mayor of New York; Jesse Jackson—these individuals have never, in the course of their political careers, ever mentioned the existence of Black political prisoners in the United States. They have never demanded that they be freed. Yet when Mandela made his walk to freedom, David Dinkins invited him to the United States, to New York; he talked about how it was a great moment for every African-American—and it was. Jesse Jackson flew to South Africa to be the man-of-the-moment, the man on the scene at the historical moment. But again, there are scores of Black political prisoners right here in the United States and none of these leaders are talking about them.

My point is that nineteen years of isolation, and nineteen years of negation of what you have stood for and fought for, take their toll on an individual. So when I see Nelson Mandela step out of a prison in South Africa I imagine how he must have felt—he must have felt a great joy at seeing his people continuing their struggle for freedom, and paying him homage for his strength and his consistency. But he also must have felt a great sadness about having had his life snatched from him because he decided to stand up for what was right, and what was truthful. So in a lot of respects, I feel that same type of ambivalence. People ask me, "Are you bitter that you spent nineteen years in prison?" and I think bitterness is an inappropriate word. I have mixed feelings about it, but it was something that came as a consequence of taking a position, and taking positions as a Black person, in a racist society. And I had to accept that.

In Defense of Self-Defense

Black Panther Party Executive Mandate #1

The Black Panther Party for Self-Defense calls upon the American people in general and the Black people in particular to take careful note of the racist California Legislature, which is now considering legislation aimed at keeping the Black people disarmed and powerless at the very same time that racist police agencies throughout the country are intensifying the terror, brutality, murder and repression of Black people. At the same time that the American government is waging a racist war of genocide in Vietnam, the concentration camps in which Japanese Americans were interned during World War II are being renovated and expanded. Since America has historically reserved the most barbaric treatment for nonwhite people, we are forced to conclude that these concentration camps are being prepared for Black people, who are determined to gain their freedom by any means necessary.

The enslavement of Black people from the very beginning of this country, the genocide practiced on the American Indians and the con-

fining of the survivors on reservations, the savage lynching of thousands of Black men and women, the dropping of atomic bombs on Hiroshima and Nagasaki, and now the cowardly massacre in Vietnam, all testify to the fact that towards people of color the racist power structure of America has but one policy: repression, genocide, terror and the big stick.

Black people have begged, prayed, petitioned, demonstrated and everything else to get the racist power structure of America to right the wrongs which have historically been perpetrated against Black people. All of these efforts have been answered by more repression, deceit and hypocrisy. As the aggression of the racist American government escalates in Vietnam, the police agencies of America escalates the repression of Black people throughout the ghettos of America. Vicious police dogs, cattle prods and increased patrols have become familiar sights in Black communities. City Hall turns a deaf ear to the pleas of Black people for relief from this increasing terror.

The Black Panther Party for Self-Defense believes that the time has come for Black people to arm themselves against this terror before it is too late. The pending Mulford Act brings the hour of doom one step nearer. A people who have suffered so much for so long at the hands of a racist society must draw the line somewhere. We believe that the Black communities of America must rise up as one man to halt the progression of a trend that leads inevitably to their total destruction.

Huey P. Newton

Toward Rethinking Self-Defense in a Racist Culture

Black Survival in a United States in Transition

Power most often costs more than it's worth; the man who attains power, not knowing its proper use, loses it in the end, for all that is held by power will some day revolt.

(Notes from unstruck music)

Conventional wisdom holds that peaceful and non-violent change is in the ultimate best interest of a social system. Seldom is the use of force seen as socially productive. By and large this is true. Regardless of the causes, very few civilizations have survived cataclysmic violent internal upheavals, or the long-term decay of their institutions of social control (which amounts to the same thing, for institutional decay results in unreasonable resort to force and repression, thereby causing violent social reaction). If a society thrives through peaceful change, then the exercise of power must be perceived as "just" or at least indicative of a common moral identity. No status-quo power can long maintain itself without some claim to moral integrity unless it does so by use of naked force, and history illustrates that force alone is insufficient to maintain and hold power.

When we rethink the concept of "self-defense" against racist aggression we are also reevaluating the ethical grounds for the use of force in a particular social context. Any concept of "legal" force is determined by the prevailing ideas of those who govern the use of violence.

In U.S. society these prevailing ideas are erected upon the notion of white-skin privilege, that is, of European superiority. This notion holds that a white person's life is somehow intrinsically worth more than the life of a person of color. This, of course, has played itself out in history. The genocide of Native Americans, the establishment of the African slave trade, and the subsequent era of European colonialism all testify to the fact that white-skin privilege ideologically justified the use of violence in pursuit of European profit and control over people of color. This is the context in which Black people must discuss the idea of self-defense. No rational discussion of self-defense for Black people can proceed without at least this basic understanding.

Perhaps it would be useful to further examine the relationship of force to the American national character, and how this relationship has been institutionalized. Very few people can argue, with any credibility, that the establishment of the United States was a non-violent historical episode. The seizure of the North American land mass from its native population was a decidedly genocidal undertaking. The consistency of this enterprise over such a long period of time—over 250 years—refutes any notion that European racism was merely the aberration of a particular era. The use of African chattel slave labor to establish the foundation for the great North American economic and industrial "miracle" was steeped in ruthless cruelty and maintained by the omnipresent threat of violence. It is estimated by some historians that over 20 million Native Americans were killed by European settlers of the Western hemisphere between the 15th and 19th centuries, and that over 50 million Africans died in the middle passage between Africa and the Americas in the period between the sixteenth and nineteenth centuries. In the early 20th century, the projection of U.S. power into Central America, the Caribbean and elsewhere proceeded in the wake of gunboats or relied upon the bayonets of U.S. Marines. Indeed, the U.S. has invaded Central America over two dozen times in the last century, and has annexed territories it seized from other European colonial powers defeated in "just wars."

In the words of a 1960s activist, "violence is as American as apple pie." Force and violence are part of the American male "folk wisdom" that socializes generations of white males into macho notions of aggression toward people of color. One small example of this is the cliché that the West was "won" by the six-shooter. Indeed, the sanctimonious glorification of equality based upon force could be summed up in a play on the words of the U.S. Declaration of Independence which states that "all men are created equal." A popular saying on the 19th-century frontier was that "God may have created men, but Sam Colt made 'em equal," Sam Colt, of course, being the reknowned American gun-maker and founder of Colt Firearms Corporation. Flowing out of the notions of white-skin privilege and the white-male "frontier mentality" is the subconscious presumption (now normative for white American cultural ethics) that all Europeans have a moral right, even a responsibility, to use force whenever their position is threatened, and that people of color have no equivalent moral right to defend themselves from European aggression—especially when the aggression is cloaked under the name of "law and order" or U.S. "national interest."

When we witness the countless incidents of racist police brutality and murder that are an everyday feature of the Black experience in the U.S., or the use of U.S. military force in Nicaragua, Grenada, Panama and the Persian Gulf, it is evident that there is a double standard when it comes to the use of violence: one standard for Europeans and another for people of color. It has been said that "patriotism is the last refuge of a scoundrel." Perhaps it can be said as well that racism is the first refuge of the insecure. Racism, having exercised considerable influence in the development of western nation-states, has built into these states this dual standard of humanity, which is so ingrained that it is often taken for granted. As a consequence, "freedom" for the national "racial" minority, as a whole, often requires the radical disruption of the social status quo and a complete reevaluation of the dominant values and norms. It is little wonder therefore that the demand for human rights by the victims of racist subjugation is always perceived by the dominant culture as unreasonable and threatening. Nowhere is this better illustrated than around the issue of force, as it relates to self-defense against racist violence.

In the United States, poor people and especially African-Americans are universally encouraged to pursue non-violence in their struggle for human rights. It is argued on the one hand that "violence" *per se* is unproductive and only begets more violence, and, on the other hand, that "you can't win anyway." "You" of course being the poor person of a darker hue. Subsidized by "liberal" foundation grants, institutions exist to train the poor in non-violent attitudes and actions. The mainstream media, decidedly male and white, while bombarding the populace with esoteric violence in the form of cop shows and Rambo movies, send the subliminal message to the white male population that the use of force and violence by underclass African-American and Third World peoples is by its very nature either criminal or morally suspect. African-American history is rewritten to emphasize the "non-violent" struggle for human and civil rights, while equally heroic but violent examples of struggle are pigeon-holed and dismissed.

Even the history of "non-violent" activism in the African-American struggle for "equality" is presented in a sterile light. The Reverend Martin Luther King, Jr. is consistently portrayed by the mainstream white media and in American history books as a toothless moral dreamer who essentially endorsed the proposition of the American capitalist state and its support of reactionary movements around the world. Of course nothing is further from the truth. Clearly, "non-violence" as preached by the mainstream media to Black Americans and the poor is never put forward as a tactic, but as a goal in itself.

While the disenfranchised Black community is fed the psychological pablum of non-violence, the enfranchised majority white community trains its children in the use of force in its war colleges and police paramilitary institutions. Moreover, Eurocentric American nationalism provides the mass culture with a moral and ethical framework in which to act out the violent impulses of their institutional training. The tradition of "conservatism" and the "right" are fundamental standards by which all other perceptions and views are measured. Thus an unfair imbalance is achieved between the benefactors of a racist society and its underclass. Indeed, the so-called "liberal" American tradition operates within this race- and class-bound imbalance, which is one reason why the so-called "two-party" (Democrat–Republican) body politic and the principle of separate branches of government are bankrupt, and never prevented U.S. intervention in the Third World, e.g., Korea, the Congo, Vietnam, Grenada, Angola, the Middle East, Libya and Central America, and it never secured for African-Americans equal and fair treatment under existent law.

The obvious consequence of a dual standard of human expectation is a unique system of democratic fascism and a permanent condition of police or military repression aimed at the underclass and social dissidents. Limited political "democracy" is permitted while corporate control of the economy dictates the real content and direction of the state. In this context the specter of racist subjugation resolves itself in an ongoing and continuous cycle of police repression, underclass crime and social deprivation—in other words a permanent state of crisis.

The highest expression of this system of democratic fascism appears to be the "National Security State," or NSS. This Orwellian corporate government structure has developed both as a corporate political manager of, and a reaction to, the condition of permanent domestic social crisis and an insurgent post-colonial Third World. The American NSS, as an institution, sponsors and sanctions racist violence of "law enforcement" at home and euphemistic "low-intensity conflict" in the Third World. In terms of its breadth of organization and its management of violence as an instrument of policy, the NSS is the ultimate purveyor of force on the face of the earth.

The bureaucracy and technocrats of the NSS serve the transnational interests of corporate America. It derives its strength and power from control of technology, a huge military-police apparatus, and its capacity to control the primary sources of information. Because the NSS sees itself as preserving "the American way of life," i.e. status quo power, it views its own citizens as subversive to "national security" whenever they disagree with the police or the interests of the NSS. Consequently "law enforcement" takes on a decidedly political function. Behind criminal law enforcement lurk the political police whose job it is to contain the unruly, quiet the outspoken, and destroy the dreamers of a new order. Effective mass organization of people against racist/class inequality, against high minority unemployment, against socio-economic dislocation (homelessness), or for the redistribution of wealth, reorganization of national priorities, and social control of technology, is always seen by the NSS as disruptive of the status quo. For this basic reason, essentially moral and economic issues such as street crime, drug abuse, criminal justice, or the the African-American "underclass" are political campaign issues gratuitously used to manufacture an ill-informed public consensus which endorses "democratic" repression of dissent and of the disenfranchised, as the Willie Horton issue was used by the racist right during the 1988 presidential campaign. An accurate assessment of the use of violence against minorities in a racist culture would be very difficult if African-Americans did not take a serious look at the nature of the National Security State.

Covert Action Information Bulletin, a Washington, D.C.-based non-profit civilian watchdog organization, recently reported the existence of the little-known "State Defense Forces" (SDFs) being created throughout America. According to *CAIB,* these "State Defense Forces" (a generic term) have been organized in approximately twenty-four states as auxiliaries to the already legally constituted state National Guard. It is presumed that a domestic SDF will be needed to control dissent and civil unrest in the event of a national emergency arising out of an unpopular U.S. military invasion abroad in which the National Guard is federalized and sent overseas. Recruits for the SDFs are unpaid civilians, and though it appears that anyone can join the SDF, its ranks are at present filled by zealots of the political right. This is significant, especially for African-Americans who are considered by the NSS to be an acute threat to America's "domestic security" by virtue of the justice of their grievances. It should come as little surprise to know that the SDF cadres are being trained in urban riot and crowd control, and in the use of weapons such as shotguns, M-16s, M-60s and 45-caliber pistols, as well as in various police techniques of anti-insurgency. While African-Americans are being taught, trained and indoctrinated into a non-violent frame of mind, the white American National Security State is teaching, training and indoctrinating its adherents to employ lethal force in suppression of dissent and protest. This is not a coincidence. The violent mentality of the racist status quo and the white fear of Black America are almost symbiotic in nature. This seeming symbiosis has as its objective the denigration of the political option of self-defense for people of color, and the criminalization of the advocacy of such options. Thus, people of color are encouraged to rely on the very system of violence that subjugates them.

In January of 1989, Don Jackson, a Black police officer on leave from the Hawthorne, California police department drove through predominantly white Long Beach, California on a personal fact-finding mission. He was investigating reports of racist police harrassment. Mr. Jackson was shadowed during his drive by an unmarked KNBC-TV van. What happened to Mr. Jackson was nationally televised in graphic detail: he was stopped arbitrarily by policemen from Long Beach, one of whom slammed his head through a plate glass window to impress upon him exactly who was boss. Mr. Jackson wrote in a January 23rd *New York Times* op-ed article, "Police Embody Racism to My People," that police brutality inflicted on Black people has a greater historical function than mere gratuitous violence:

The black American finds that the most prominent reminder of his second-class citizenship is the police. In the history of this country, police powers were collectively shared among whites regarding black people. A slave wandering off the plantation could be stopped and detained by any white person who saw fit to question his purpose for being away from home... A variety of stringent laws were enacted and enforced to stamp the imprint of inequality on the black American. *It has long been the role of the police to see that the plantation mentality is passed from one generation of blacks to another.* No one has enforced these rules with more zeal than the police. (emphasis added)

The irony of Mr. Jackson's assessment is that the "collectively shared" police powers of whites has given way to a collectively shared perception of Black people as potential criminals and terrorists. Indeed, even Mr. Jackson's effort to expose the truth fell victim to the need for white society to obscure it. The dramatic racist police mistreatment of Mr. Jackson was juxtaposed on national news broadcasts next to Black people "looting" white and immigrant Hispanic-owned stores in Miami. The white media, as if by reflex, played to the dual realities of a racist culture. Surely white America got the message that the police have their hands full dealing with potentially volatile Blacks, and that if they are somewhat aggressive, who can really blame them? At the same time, Blacks were made to feel as if their truth was being told. The duality of historical experiences—one Black, one white—

whatever the facts, makes "democratic" consensus without equal power impossible.

Equal power? What does this mean for African-Americans? Perhaps we would do well to reevaluate our idea of what equality means, for if we are of the notion that individual freedom in a racist culture can be acquired at the expense of the collective freedom of the victims of that culture, then we have accepted the amoral concept of "equal opportunity exploitation," the very same concept that enslaved our ancestors and which divides the world today into two antagonistic divisions of "haves" and "have nots," exploited and exploiter. Malcolm X once said "history is the best subject to reward all research." There is no way we can judge the relationship between African-Americans and European-Americans under imagined conditions of equal power, that is, absent our history of subjugation, absent the consequences of chattel enslavement driven by profit incentive, or regardless of the elaborate edifice of legal and social discrimination erected to maintain African-Americans in a purely "minority" status in which their interests are subsumed by the interest of the dominant caste and class. The common humanity of both African-Americans and whites has had to endure and suffer the predatory appetite of a system devised to enrich the few at the expense of the many. Whatever episodic sparks of humanity that the races may have exhibited toward each other surely occurred despite the European nation-state system—not because of it. The struggle for Black empowerment can ill afford to ignore history. There is no power without the capacity for independent self-defense.

Whenever the question of Black self-defense arises, it inevitably stumbles over the issues of "legality" and "appropriateness of violence" (which all too often amount to the same thing, that is, violence is always considered appropriate if—and only if—it is "legal"). This is because self-defense against racist attack is generally viewed in a very narrow fashion which is unjustified by our experience as a people. To combat this, in the first place, the idea of the use of force to defend oneself has to be stripped of racist duality. Secondly, we have to understand the function of force as the European power elite perceive it, and third, we must evaluate the utility of a newly derived definition of self-defense in assuring collective survival.

Should we examine Mr. Jackson's historical assessment of police violence we would see that it is the same as the organization of racist terrorism. Violence was historically used in conjunction with other psychological factors to dehumanize the African slaves and secure their system of servitude. For the men who controlled this system, slave control was not only an economic consideration but a matter of physical self-defense as well. The fear of Native Americans and of African slave revolt were two permanent features of early European-American colonial life. In 1710, the governor of Virginia, Alexander Spotswood, advised the Virginia Assembly in these words:

> Freedom wears a cap which can, without a tongue, call together all those who long to shake off the fetters of slavery, and as such an insurrection would surely be attended with most dreadful consequences, so I think we cannot be too early in providing against it, both by putting ourselves in a better posture of defense and making a law to prevent the consultations of Negroes.

Apparently the honorable governor's advice did not fall on deaf ears because the Virginia slave code mandated that should a slave run away and not immediately return, "anyone whosoever may kill or destroy such slaves by such means as he shall think fit." In addition the courts had authority to order dismemberment or any other measure "as they in their discretion shall think fit, for the reclaiming of any such incorrigible slave, and terrifying others from like practices." Other examples abound of the terroristic use of violence codified into law with the express purpose of maintaining our ancestors in a position of abject fear and servitude. If times have changed, the residual and accumulative benefits of white-skin privilege still ensure the legal codification of violence in maintenance of the status quo. It is this status quo, with all the moral righteousness of the founding fathers behind it, that now preaches against the evils of terrorism. Former President Ronald Reagan admitted to a profound historical analogy when he equated the terrorist and murderous CIA-backed Nicaraguan "Contras" to the "moral equivalent of America's founding fathers." To borrow a phrase from the distinguished Governor Spotswood of Virginia, African-Americans would do well by putting themselves in "a better posture of defense."

The purpose in drawing attention to early American history is not to revel in moral self-righteousness or engage in useless judgement of another period when behavior and attitudes were determined by different standards than today. It should not be too difficult to see that the "founding fathers" of America were men of property driven by the contradictions of European culture, a culture based on agriculture, with feudal hierarchies of the nobility (lords), vassals and peasants, which evolved from the slave societies of Greece and Rome. History is clear: erected upon the European conquest of North

America, upn the genocide of the Indians and the racist brutality of slavery, Europeans stratified a civilization based on private property. The European need for land and space, combined with the dubious ethics of mercantile capitalism, made racism and genocide integral to the society and system we know today. The rhapsody of the American dream sold to countless immigrants is only a part of the true story. We must understand the truth of our historical experience so that we are clear in our thinking and fully appreciate what America is capable of.

Racism has been an important tool in dividing the poor and working peoples of America. It has prevented white laborers, the middle class, and various Third World immigrant communities from uniting against an exploitative and relatively small white male elite. Despite this objective "function" of racism it would be inappropriate for the African-American to ignore the very real physical threat racism represents to our empowerment. In the struggle for power, often perception is more important than reality. The common Eurocentric perception of African-Americans is that they lack certainty of principle and a willingness to defend themselves. Our self-destructive treatment of each other, that is, our obsessive imitation of the most shallow white American values, our disregard for Black youth, "Black on Black crime" and the entire range of psychotic self-hatred we act out every day in our social relations reinforce white Americans with negative perceptions of Black people. Many of the problems that now confront African-Americans begin at home, in our community. Until we establish independent mechanisms of community supervision that provide moral, ethical, political and social direction, African-Americans will continue to be the doormat of U.S. society. Depending on outside forces to regulate and govern the African-American community is a prescription for disaster. A community without *internal* authority and control is no community at all.

Weakness tempts power to practice brutality and oppression. The seeming increase of so-called "racially motivated attacks" is in large part the consequence of the apparent inability or unwillingness of Black America to defend itself. While the term "racially motivated attack" is a media buzzword intended to individualize systemic racist subjugation, we need not fall victim to this deception. There is nothing exceptional or individual about racist attack in a racist society. Media buzzwords notwithstanding, our response to racist attack must be collective, uncompromising and most of all organized! We should respond in a political manner to all racist attack, as well as to conditions that invite attacks. Both legal racist violence (police, state and institutional brutality) and extra-legal racist violence (racist gang violence, individual discriminatory treatment) serve the same function: the subjugation of the targeted racial national minority. Black people must break with the mental baggage of slavery and shed the knee-jerk "non-threatening negro" posture white folks love so well. Our concept of force, its political utility, is obsolete. Force and violence must be seen for what they are and placed in a relevant political context: instruments of political power, instruments of control.

The violence of racist oppression, when internalized by the African-American community, results in reactionary violence or negative violence, and it must be repressed by the African community if self-defense is to advance beyond vigilantism. Vigilantism is not the political organization of force—it is the social organization of civilian frustration. It can be co-opted by the status quo, misdirected by opportunists, and will eventually fizzle out. The political organization of force by the Black community implies its connection to the struggle for power and control over the entire quality of life available to Black people. Unlike reactionary apolitical violence, or vigilante force, the concept of Black self-defense, e.g. the political organization of force, is *proactive* force. Self-defense in this context is as broad as the requirements of and the struggle for empowerment. Legality and illegality are relative to the struggle for empowerment—not sacrosanct in and of themselves. White folks taught us the efficacy of this approach to this use of force.

By way of example, the tactic of economic boycott can be seen as an economic form of self-defense against economic exploitation, injustice or discrimination—especially when it upsets the colonial relationship between the African-American community and the status quo power. In this sense it is proactive and not reactive. Taking control of social institutions or educational systems that affect the quality of African-American life by establishment political means, i.e. electoral politics, and the creation of grassroots alternative institutions which provide services to the Black community are forms of proactive self-defense, for a primary objective of self-defense is deterrence, and a limited political power is better than no power at all. But it is not always enough to deter racist attack.

Black Americans can never relinquish the right to exert a political consequence on those institutions and individuals who abuse us. Questions of "legality" and "illegality" are relative—the appropriateness is both tactical and ethical. Insofar as Black America is unable to punish racist brutality and exert a political consequence for racist attack we are weak, vulnerable and unequal. It is a moral imperative to organize Black people to defend themselves. We must get away from the plantation mentality and the cowardly notion that organizing force in defense of Black people and in pursuit of our political objectives, when necessary, is somehow amoral and therefore rightly illegal. All people have the right to defend themselves. Moreover, all that is legal is not morally just.

The proper criterion for distinguishing between "right" and "wrong" is not mysterious. It is embodied in the principles that advance the cause of the oppressed and exploited over the cause of those who live by oppression and exploitation. Even though the oppressed and exploited may not always be "correct," their cause is just and right. Nor should we foolishly imagine that, by following the guidance and leadership of those who uphold the cause of the oppressed, we are somehow conferring favors on such leadership. For leadership is a burden—surely the more one knows, the more one is responsible for. This is why current Black leaders act like they don't know what's happening in times of crisis, because white folks will hold them responsible for the consciousness of the masses. Our leaders must be responsible to us—not to the status quo, which demands that our people remain in check.

Humankind has a weakness for falsehood, vanity and crookedness, not because we are inured to truth and selfless devotion to community, but because it is much easier to pursue falsehood and vanity than to seek truth and social responsibility. So it is, that the delusions of the material world gratify us and yet leave an aching emptiness in our soul. Perhaps this weakness is why African-Americans, in the tradition of Western materialism, would much rather follow a fool dressed in a silk suit than a wise righteous person draped in rags. We fold our hearts like a handkerchief, tucking it away in our back pocket, sitting on it as if embarrassed that we possess a heart at all. Surely the corruption of a person's heart is a great tragedy—for the malaise of the human spirit is reflected in the social condition of a people. Their need arises from the drifting and unfocused hunger of Black America for a class of men, women and youth committed to upholding the social, moral, ethical and spiritual integrity of our community—no matter how great the sacrifice. We need to care more about ourselves than about what white folks think about us, and in so doing realize that "history does not respond to those who lack the basic instruments of bringing about historical change." This means we must acquire independent power. The rhetoric of "liberalism," "left" dogma, or "right" integrationist accomodation are passé, obsolete. They are without moral or ethical integrity and of limited utility to Black America in crisis. The crisis of Black America is not only material (i.e. economic), or political, or even social. It is at its root a malaise of the heart—of the spirit. The reality of the nation-state in which we live is in transition. Our struggle for liberation as a people must reflect this and invigorate us with a new sense of direction and purpose.

The world is changing. It is in a transition from a world order dominated by European economic hegemony born out of racist colonialism to one in which that system of domination is under increasing strain to accomodate the interests of the disenfranchised. Increasing awareness of the need for a world order and redistribution of wealth unencumbered by selfish class-based nationalism is rising in the world. Technology has placed humankind at the crossroads of history. What will be Black America's role in the historic struggles that lie ahead? Black leaders who do not frame the struggle in this context are not Black leaders at all.

While we must prepare ourselves collectively to wage many struggles at once, we must do so with a common sense of mission and purpose. Without this sense of mission and purpose we will succumb to the spiritual and material degradation of a racist culture. The times in which we live portend both hope and doom. During the long centuries of the slave-trade, Africans had a sense of mission, of common purpose—to survive and defeat the brutal system of dehumanization and "break de' chains." In post-Reconstruction America, when the national agenda was set for the remainder of the century by putting "Negroes" back in their place as neo-serfs (sharecroppers) and servants, Black people had a sense of collective mission. When white labor was bludgeoned into submission by the robber barons of commerce, and the political elites of both North and South consolidated the economic wealth of America into the greatest material growth in human history, Black people had a sense of mission, purpose and common direction which culminated in the upheavals of the early- and mid-twentieth century for civil and human rights. We must rekindle this flame and sense of purpose, but on a much higher level. We know what white America is capable of when it comes to people of color. We understand the limitations and imperatives of history, and a racist culture. The question therefore is what do we intend to do about it.

The Cutting Edge
of Prison Technology

Q: To compare the situation of prisoners in European jails with those in the US, could you give your impression of your visit to prisoners from the Red Army Faction earlier this year (Irmgard, Christine, Gunter, Helmut and Lutz).

Dhoruba Bin Wahad: In Europe, the idea of political prisoners is something that is established. Most governments admit that there are people in prison as a consequence of their political agenda and activities in opposition to state policies. The United States does not make such an admission. The United States maintains that there are no political prisoners and that the only people in prison are those who have committed crimes. That official position is, of course, mirrored by the media and by the various institutions in U.S. society. Because of that decision the treatment of political prisoners, and the way they are singled out for special treatment, goes unreported. Political prisoners in the United States by and large are subjected to isolation from other prisoners, from their families and communities. They tend to be sent to the remotest prisons in the U.S. They are constantly harassed under the pretext of having violated the institution's rules. They are set up by the

An interview given in East Germany in February 1981, subsequent to a lecture at the University of Berlin.

prison officials either to be brutally assaulted, placed in isolation, or even recharged on fabricated criminal charges. So the conditions I saw during my brief visits with the German political prisoners, and in talking with them, mirrors some of the conditions that political prisoners in the United States have been subjected to.

Q: Particularly in the matter of solitary confinement?

DBW: Yes. The United States has been on a campaign these last 15 years or so, to refine and develop conditions of solitary confinement. Every state in the United States is developing, or has already established, what are called maximum security prisons. That is, a prison within a prison, designed to house a small number of prisoners that the state deems as incorrigible or as threats. Almost all the political prisoners in the U.S.—and there are over 150, the majority of them Black—are in some type of maximum security confinement and in what we call maxi-maxi prisons.

Q: Is there any direct correlation between the situation and treatment of prisoners in Europe, specifically West Germany, with those in the USA? Is there a coordinated policy in this area? Is it the result of the conference held in Puerto Rico in 1978 which representatives from European states as well as from the U.S. attended? Susan Rosenberg identifies this as being central to the consolidation of policy and the formation of the Joint Anti-Terrorist Task Force.

DBW: Yes. The coordination of policies between the United States and other governments subjected to Western influence is part and parcel of an overall coordination of military and political goals. According to the *Journal of World Nations,* 51 states employ abduction and assassination of its citizens, 115 states resort to torture and brutality in their prisons, and 125 states employ arbitrary police and legal action against its dissidents. Over 15% of the earth's peoples, 750 million to be exact, live under the rule of military regimes. Now the primary trainer of these military regimes, the primary organ of support given to these repressive policies, comes from Washington, D.C.

In the U.S. in particular, political prisoners became a matter of government policy in 1971 as a consequence of a militant Black liberation movement. One of the highlights of this policy was, of course, the assassination of the reknowned writer and political activist, George Jackson. He was murdered in San Quentin prison in August of 1971, shot to death. Officials claim he was trying to escape. A number of prison guards were killed. Documents that surfaced under the Freedom of Information Act subsequently showed that George Jackson was a target of the Counterintelligence Program aimed at the Black Panther Party.

George Jackson's murder by the California Adult Authority, the prison system, marked a change in state policy towards political activists who were in prison. This change was codified in a program known as Operation PRISAC—that's an acronym for "prison activists"—instituted in 1973–1974. The government has said that this was terminated in 1976 but we have information that indicates it was continued under a different name up until the 1980's. Operation PRISAC was designed to monitor political activists who were brought to prison as a consequence of the Counterintelligence Program. In 1973–74 the federal government invited all the heads of the various state prison systems to Washington to coordinate their policies in dealing with political prisoners, because this was a different breed of prisoner, a person that had to be isolated and neutralized. It's interesting to note that PRISAC became a necessity because the Counterintelligence Program was so successful in framing political activists. Once these activists—most of them were to become Black political prisoners—were taken off the streets, then a new program had to be designed to isolate them in prison, and monitor the activities of people coming out of prison who may have been influenced through their contact with them. Between 1973 and 1976, many of those who were politicized in prison were mysteriously murdered. To this day no one has been brought to justice for these murders. One individual that comes prominently to mind is a man by the name of Charles Rabbi Parker. He was a well-known political activist in the New York State prison system who had become a member of the Black Panther Party while in prison. He had organized hundreds of prisoners into unions, into a People's Party, he was a leader in the Attica (prison) rebellion in 1971. He was eventually let out of prison in 1976 and by 1978 he had been murdered— mysteriously. People in Europe should understand that the development of political repression in the United States is reflective of the cooptation and the neutralization of legitimate movements for social change, whether it's the anti-war movement that arose out of the Vietnam War, the Black civil rights or Black liberation movement, or the Puerto Rican nationalist movement, the U.S. has carried out a policy of repression, trained other governments in the use of repressive tactics and established a network—a working relationship with the various law enforcement apparatuses in the other states—especially in Europe.

Q: Could you compare the conditions that you had to endure for 19 years with those of the West German political prisoners who have also had to endure similar conditions for the same period of time?

DBW: When I visited the German political prisoners earlier this year many of them reported that they had spent years in isolation, in sensory deprivation conditions. On their initial capture and for long periods thereafter they were isolated from each other and from all human contact. Their legal visits were monitored, their social visits curtailed and restricted. Their families were harassed after visits. All this of course struck a familiar cord with me because I have endured the same thing. I spent seven years off and on in isolation, solitary confinement. In the United States isolation basically means 23 hours a day confinement to a cell, which is generally 8 feet by 10 feet in size. It's usually a steel cell with a cot, a steel shelf bolted to the wall. When I first went to prison—and I must point out that it was a state prison in New York State, as opposed to a federal prison—every prison had an isolation unit. It was called disciplinary segregation and during the course of my confinement the Department of Correction changed the criteria for confining a prisoner in disciplinary segregation to meet its political needs, to deal with political prisoners.

Q: Was the Marion County prison the model prison for this kind of confinement?

DBW: The prison at Marion, Illinois has become a model for what's called isolation units or maximum security surveillance units, which came about as a consequence of a series of lectures and meetings by very important figures in the field of psychology and behavior modification. The United States government is very much "into" the development of techniques, ideas and principles for modifying a person's behavior through sensory deprivation. They have carried out these experiments in many prisons, and Marion, Illinois was the major laboratory for this. The prisoners there are isolated 23.5 hours a day. They are subjected to brutal treatment by prison guards. Many of the prisoners cannot have social visits, they have no personal property to speak of. They are forced to watch television 23.5 hours a day. Investigations have shown that the water system in Marion, which the prisoners drink from, is infected by toxic waste, and the prisoners have been developing various degrees of blood cancer and other ailments, to the point where the prison guards and the prison officals don't drink the water from the prison system. The majority of political prisoners there are Black political prisoners and Puerto Rican nationalist prisoners. They are kept, of course, in the special housing unit, the isolation unit. Many of them have been there for years.

Q: In 1979 you were transferred to what was called Unit 14 at Clinton Prison. What did that mean for you?

DBW: Well, before the construction of the Shawanga Correctional Facility in New York State, which is modelled after the Marion prison, the New York State prison officals did not have a maximum-maximum security prison to house political prisoners.

Q: You mean a prison within a prison?

DBW: That's correct. So what they did was to identify a few of the most notorious segregation units that they had as places where they would put political prisoners. And Unit 14 was one of these places.

Q: Can these be compared with what are called the dead-tracts in West German prisons, prisons within prisons?

DBW: That's correct. Every prison in New York State now has a prison within a prison, and New York State has built two maximum-maximum security prisons. The first one was in Sullivan County, New York, where as we speak there are five Black political prisoners. Shawanga is unique in the sense that the prisoners' activities are monitored 24-hours-a-day. There are surveillance cameras on the prison gallery, the prison hallway, the prison tier, which the cells open up onto, and the camera moves down the gallery on a track, it's a remote camera. The cell doors are opened by remote control whenever the prisoners are let out of their cells into the close supervision unit and an officer follows them around with a clipboard recording everything they do, every word they say. I guess in comparison to Marion this would be seen as liberal because in Marion the prisoners do not even come out of their cells. But the U.S. government is building another prison in Colorado which will open next year and is being touted as the cutting edge of prison technology. It will use robotics, robots taking care of the prisoners. There will be no human contact between prisoners and guards, even. Unless, of course, they are to be assaulted by them. The prisoners will be locked in their cells 23 hours a day. This prison is employing every means of technology to accomplish this end, and the United States government is very proud of its efforts.

Q: Where does the Lexington (Kentucky) Unit fit into this whole structure?

DBW: The federal system did not have a maximum-maximum security facility for women, and because a significant number of the political prisoners, especially the white, North American, anti-imperialist political prisoners and Puerto Rican political prisoners were women, the U.S. government had a problem. I think they only had two or three federal women's penitentiaries in the U.S. and only one of them was seriously a maximum security prison. So what they did was to take Lexington, which was a prison hospital, and convert a section of it into a maximum security unit for women. They painted this unit all white, they removed any type of sensory stimulation from the environment. The guards were instructed that these individuals were very dangerous terrorists and three women were brought there to "open up" the unit. One was Susan Rosenberg, another Alejandrina Torres, and the other was Silvia Baraldini. What they did not anticipate though was that people on the outside would mobilize against this blatant attempt to isolate political activists, torture them, and bring about their demise by means of sensory deprivation. A campaign was mounted by progressive people and progressive forces to close the Lexington Control Unit. This unit was visited by Amnesty International and other Human Rights Organizations and it was declared, just as the Marion facility was, to be inhumane and to be an institution dedicated to the torture of human beings. Under this national and international pressure, the United States government was forced to close the Lexington Control Unit. However, they only closed it after they had developed an alternative unit in Mariana, Florida. Of course, two of the women who were in the Lexington Unit were ultimately transferred to this maxi-maxi prison in Mariana, Florida, again modelled after Marion, Illinois, where they remain today.

Q: On the matter of Amnesty International, they have been singularly lacking—certainly in Europe, and in West Germany in particular—in terms of the situation of political prisoners during the last 20 years. Why?

DBW: This goes to the heart of the issue as to why in the U.S. progressive people and political activists had to develop the Campaign to Free Black Political Prisoners and Prisoners of War in the United States. Amnesty International, Americas Watch, and these so-called human rights organizations do not deal with the politics of resistance that typifies the political prisoners today in the West.

In the United States there are 30 million Black people, but very few people in Europe understand that those people have a particular history, and this history is one of domestic colonialism, internal colonialism. There is a struggle going on in the United States to empower masses of Black people. And the United States government has done everything in its power to sidetrack that struggle, to destroy its most militant advocates, to prop up certain elements in the Black community who support racism and the idea that Black people enjoy the full panoply of rights and privileges all other American citizens enjoy, but simply suffer from social discrimination. In the United States, every aspect of political repression, of racism, has historically been bolstered by the legal system and the law. It was the law that said that Black people were three-fifths of a human being—it was in the Constitution of the United States. When Black people were enslaved, slavery was legal. With Jim Crow, the U.S. version of segregation and apartheid was established after the Civil War, and again it was codified in law. In the United States, Black people's struggle has been at once legal and extra-legal. This is why Black political prisoners in the U.S. are so isolated. People do not understand that the law is used to destroy the legitimate political aspirations of people of color.

Here we come face to face with the contradiction of Amnesty International's policies. Amnesty International does not support movements that advocate the overthrow of the existing political order. What it means is that even if a political order is racist and reactionary, historically discriminatory, the victims have no right to carry out acts of violence against that state. Amnesty International's policies have led it to the ignoble position of not supporting political prisoners in the United States. In fact it did not recognize Nelson Mandela, clearly an individual who was in prison because of his political views and his struggle against the apartheid regime in South Africa.

Q: Are you saying there are also problems of race in the attitude of the representatives of that organization?

DBW: Yes. Amnesty International is a racist organization. It's a Eurocentric organization. It's an organization that does not believe that Black people, or people of color, have a legitimate right to struggle against established states by any means necessary.

Q: It's been the experience of the relatives and lawyers of the West German prisoners that they have knocked on a door that's never opened.

DBW: That's been our experience too. Amnesty International has only recognized one Black prisoner as a political prisoner and that is Elmer Geronimo Pratt who has been in prison for 21 years. Before him they had recognized the Wilmington 10, the Reverend Ben Chaves and these political prisoners. But other than that, Amnesty International has not dealt with the cases of over 150 political prisoners in the U.S. and this is their shame. As a consequence, the prisoners themselves and the movements from which they come have had an uphill battle in gaining recognition. Our Campaign to Free Black Political Prisoners is often boycotted by particular venues. If we want to do a fund-raising benefit for political prisoners, oftentimes we are denied the use of a huge auditorium because we are not connected to organizations such as Amnesty International. When we say we are from the Campaign to Free Black Political Prisoners in the U.S., they ask us, "Is this for Amnesty International?" And when we say no they say "Well who are these prisoners? We don't have political prisoners in the United States." So Amnesty International plays the part of the legal international opposition to liberal reform in the so-called democracies and the metropoles of the West. The masses of people are not aware that their governments carry out policies of murder, of manipulation of the legal system. In the United States for instance the FBI has carried out a programme called "Operation Mirage" aimed at targeting Arab Americans in the wake of the Gulf War. Its purpose was, of course, to isolate them from the mainstream society and ultimately lock them up in the detention centers should the war have been a drawn-out affair. So we see that the federal government of the United States becomes emboldened by the failure of independent international bodies to monitor political repression.

Q: Could you talk about the number of political prisoners in the U.S., the particular groups they belong to and come from—about their prison conditions, and about those who are in the worst situations?

DBW: We have documented over 150 cases of political imprisonment in the United States, using the criteria as established by the United Nations Commision on Human Rights and the Universal Declaration of Human Rights which defines a political prisoner as an individual who, in pursuit of their political conscience, and as a consequence of their political activity, are imprisoned for those activities. The majority of the political prisoners in the United States are Black. The second largest number are Puerto Rican nationals who consider themselves prisoners-of-war because Puerto Rico is a colony of the United States. As the Universal Declaration of Human Rights makes plain, colonized people have a right to wage armed struggle against the colonizing power for their freedom, and the combatants in this struggle have to be treated as prisoners-of-war. Of course the United States does not consider Puerto Rico a colony and therefore does not treat the Puerto Rican nationalists as prisoners-of-war but rather as criminals. The third largest group of political prisoners in the United States are white anti-imperialist political prisoners. These are individuals who come from the left in the United States and who have carried out support movements, support actions, on behalf of the Black liberation movements and of the Puerto Rican nationalist movement. They have opposed U.S. intervention in the Middle East, the Caribbean, and in Latin America. These individuals are in prison also. And the fourth largest group are Native Americans from the American Indian Movement.

The majority of Black political prisoners come from the Black Panther Party or the Black Liberation Army, and the reason for this is that the majority of Black political prisoners have been in prison for the last 20 years. They were targets of the Counterintelligence Program, like Geronimo Pratt, or they were targets of Operation Newkill, like the New York 3, who were members of the Black Liberation Army, or they were targeted by the government's Joint Anti-Terrorist Task Force, like the Queens 2. Ahmed Abdul Rahman, in Detroit, has been in prison almost 20 years. He was a lieutenant in the Black Panther Party. The reason why these political prisoners are unknown in the United States, aside from the fact that the U.S. has done a magnificent job of concealing its political repression behind criminal law enforcement, is that the organization that they had been members of was destroyed by the United States government. And this is why earlier this year, after my release from prison, we established the Campaign to Free Black Political Prisoners and Prisoners-of-War in the United States. And when we talk about Black prisoners-of-war we are saying that a state of war has existed between the Black community in the United States and the racist power structure of the United States, and that this state of war has assumed many different forms. One of those forms was of course counterinsurgency. Individuals who had taken up the armed struggle, to arm the resistance agaainst racist police attacks in the Black community, and were captured as a consequence of that resistance, we define as prisoners-of-war.

Q: Could you explain a little the case of Mumia Abu-Jamal?

DBW: His is the most significant case that confronts us today in regards to Black political prisoners. Mumia Abu-Jamal was formerly the Lieutenant of Information in the Philadelphia, Pennsylvania branch of the Black Panther Party. He was an outspoken defender of the poor Black community in Philadelphia. The Philadelphia Police Department is one of the most notorious in the United States. It was headed by a former corrupt politician by the name of Frank Rizzo. The

Philadelphia P.D. had murdered and brutalized Black people for a very long time, and recently—a few years ago—this treatment burst upon the national consciousness when the Philadelphia Police Department burned down an entire area in the Black community trying to evict from a house some members of MOVE. MOVE is an organization, or a family, a group of Black activists in the Philadelphia community. Mumia Abu-Jamal was a radio announcer in Philadelphia, and a writer, who in his radio programs and his daily column supported MOVE activists in Philadelphia. He constantly reported police activities in the Black community, reported their treatment of the MOVE prisoners and the MOVE people. This resulted in an attack upon him one evening by police department officials in Philadelphia. They attacked him and his brother who was viciously beaten up by the police. In the melee, one of the police was killed and Mumia Abu-Jamal was arrested for the murder of this policeman. There was no evidence that Mumia had anything to do with the murder of this policeman. However, because of his outspoken advocacy on behalf of the MOVE people, he was put on trial for first-degree murder which is punishable by death. He has exhausted all of his legal remedies under the State and Federal law and he is now facing execution in the Pennsylvania death chamber. And so we are mounting a campaign to stop the State of Pennsylvania from murdering Mumia Abu-Jamal. Political prisoners have been murdered by the state, but all of these murders were conspiracies that were carried out behind the scenes—in dark rooms—they were carried out by officials in secret. Mumia Abu-Jamal's execution of course will not be a secret, it will be something that's codified. So if Mumia Abu-Jamal is murdered by the State of Pennsylvania, this will become a serious precedent for the actual execution, outright legal execution, of political prisoners, of political activists.

It's also useful to note that the death penalty in the United States has always been used as a means of intimidating people of color. In the U.S., 85% of the people on death row are Black, or people of color. Never in the history of the United States has a white person ever been executed for the murder of a Black person, or a person of color. Black men have been executed for rape of white women, some for rapes that were never even proven to have occurred, just on the mere allegation of the charge that they had looked at a white woman, or that they had accosted a white woman. So the death penalty in the United States has historically been used in a racist fashion. And now, if Mumia Abu-Jamal is executed it will have been used not only in a racist fashion, but in a clearly political fashion.

Q: Dr. Alan Berkman has been ill for some time. Can you detail his situation now and his state of health?

DBW: Dr. Alan Berkman was a long-time civil rights activist in the 60's. He had become increasingly militant in his support of people of color, and has made available to the various movements his expertise as a doctor. I first met Dr. Berkman when he became involved in the struggle to establish the free health clinics in the Black community and in el Barrio, the Puerto Rican ghetto in New York City. He volunteered his services to both. He went on to treat political activists and political prisoners, to go into the prisons and give independent diagnoses of political prisoners who were suffering mistreatment at the hands of the state. As a consequence of this he was targeted by the United States government. In 1982, after the Brinks expropriation operation in New York, he was summoned to appear before the Grand Jury. He went underground and was subsequently captured.

The government then said he was responsible for the treatment of Assata Shakur, a former member of the Black Panther Party who is now exiled in Cuba. They said that Dr. Berkman assisted in treating people who had been involved in the Black Liberation Army operation which resulted in Assata Shakur's escape from prison in New Jersey in 1979. He was subsequently placed in prison without charges for over two years. The government tried to coerce testimony from him in front of a Grand Jury. He refused to testify and was sent to prison, and in prison he remains. While in prison Dr. Berkman developed Parkinson's Disease. It was not diagnosed properly by prison staff. They permitted his disease to deteriorate, and he almost died. Were it not for a campaign to get medical treatment for him he would have surely died. It was made clear through subsequent interviews with Dr. Berkman that the United States government wanted him to become an informer. They wanted to use him as an example. They did not want other professionals, especially white males who are accredited by the institutions of American society, to support the causes of the Black liberation movement or the Puerto Rican nationalist movement. Dr. Berkman's health is very poor and it is doubtful whether he will ever get out of prison alive.

Q: Is it true that he has developed lymphatic cancer?

DBW: This is true, and the Bureau of Prisons has refused to allow independent doctors to treat him. This is typical policy. The same thing was done to Silvia Baraldini when she was in the Lexington Control Unit. She developed a cancer as a consequence of her treatment by the Bureau of Prisons and at first they refused to treat her. It was only because of a massive campaign to draw attention to her plight that she was ultimately taken out of the Lexington Unit and sent to another facility for treatment. Bashir Hameed, a Black political prisoner in New York State, spent over two years in solitary confinement. The express purpose was to break him physically. The New York State authorities said that he would not be let out of solitary confinement unless he renounced his political views. They viewed him as a threat because he had a considerable amount of political influence over the prison population. We had to mount a campaign for almost a year to draw attention to Bashir Hameed's plight as his health deteriorated. And we were successful. He was removed from isolation and sent to another prison.

Q: And his influence over the prison population, and its threat to the smooth running of the prison, was this because the majority of the prisoners were Black?

DBW: Yes. The prison system in the United States is a booming business. It's one of the major growth industries in the country today—even in a period of recession. In New York State for instance, 85–90% of all the prisoners are Black or Latino. And they come from only eight communities in the entire state of New York. We are talking about in excess of 50,000 prisoners. In New York state, the majority of prisons are in rural areas that are predominantly white and economically depressed, which would have enjoyed an exploitation of timber resources, of tourism, etc. The solution to this depression is to build prisons in these regions in order to employ people and bring in taxable income. A whole host of other support industries come along with the prison. In New York state over the last five years the Governor Mario Cuomo has built a new prison every 120 days. So we have a major growth industry in the trade of Black flesh for white rural employment.

The pretext that is used to fill these prisons with people of color is the war on drugs. Ninety percent of the importers of hard drugs into the United States are white males. In other words, the importation of drugs into the United States is not something that Black people are really participating in. Eighty-five percent of all the arrests in the United States on drug-related charges are of people of color, of Blacks and Latinos. So the pretext of the war on drugs gives the U.S, government the cloak of moral legitimacy in its attempts to militarize the police and erode the legal protections of its citizens. There are no longer any protections against illegal search and seizures. The police can kick in your door in the Black community now and evict people from their houses on the information that they might be dealing in drugs. There need be no fact-finding process, there need be no charges made against the people. they can just be thrown out and their houses boarded up. This is what the United States is moving towards, a system of democratic fascism.

Q: Are there any particular prisoners about whom you would like to speak?

DBW: Yes. Elmer Geronimo Pratt, who is now in Tehatchapie Prison in California. Geronimo Pratt is one of longest held Black political prisoners in the U.S. He's been in prison 21 years. The U.S. government admits to having had surveillance on Geronimo Pratt under its Counterintelligence Program, and having targeted him for neutralization. And yet, and still, he remains in prison for a murder that the United States government knows he could not have committed because he was under government surveillance in another part of the country when the murder occurred. The surveillance reports were of course destroyed by the FBI and Geronimo has remained in prison. He is a Vietnam veteran, a highly decorated veteran, and now he is suffering post-traumatic stress syndrome as a consequence of the environment of this particular prison which reminds him to a significant degree of Vietnam. He is suffering serious and severe psychological problems, and depression, which is beginning to lead to a physical deterioration.

I would also like to point out that Sekou Odinga, a Black prisoner-of-war and a former soldier in the Black Liberation Army, is in Marion, Illinois. He is beginning to suffer from the effects of physical deprivation. Sundiata Acoli, another political prisoner, is in Leavenworth federal prison along with Leonard Peltier. Tim Blunk, a white anti-imperialist political prisoner, is in Marion, Illinois.

Q: Can you tell us something more about the Mariana Facility in Miami State?

DBW: I'd like to say this about prisons in the United States. The United States does two things very well: it builds excellent prisons, and it builds military bases—very fast. In terms of prisons, it builds prisons to appear humane. The prisoners have access to television; in some cases they can make phone calls on a regular basis to family. There are visiting rooms where they can have regular visits. The food isn't all that bad. It isn't like the Tower of London 500 years ago when gruel was thrown through a slit and you were chained to a wall. What you see as a relatively clean and somewhat sterile prison environment only conceals a more pernicious type of confinement, and that is the use of sensory deprivation, the use of mind-controlling drugs, the use of behavior modification techniques. All this to bring about the deterioration of the prisoner in whole or in part. The German authorities have become very adept at it, in dealing with political prisoners, and to a lesser degree the French and the Italians. But the United States has moved into the 21st century in terms of how to control and destroy a human being.

The prisoners in Mariana are very isolated. All of their activities are monitored. Someone who has not been in prison cannot begin to understand the impact and effects of having someone watch your every activity, down to your bowel movements. The constant use of strip searches is not designed to ensure security because you are being watched 24 hours a day. They are used to humiliate someone. Probing into their body cavities is an act of rape, an act of complete dehumanization. It is done by prison staff and prison guards in an impersonal and very cold and calculated way designed to destroy your self-esteem.

Q: Which political prisoners are currently in Mariana?

DBW: There are five altogether. Puerto Rican nationalist women and white anti-imperialist prisoners.

Q: Does this include Susan Rosenberg and Silvia Baraldini?

DBW: That's correct.

Q: What about Alejandrina Torres, which prison is she now in?

DBW: She's in Alderson prison. She is very isolated there because they try to move political prisoners as far away as possible from their bases of support. For example, Sekou

Odinga is from New York, and he is being held in Marion, Illinois.

Q: I'd like to ask you about the pressures put on the relatives and the lawyers of political prisoners, the relatives who choose to visit and the lawyers who choose to represent political prisoners. What extra "attention" do they receive from the federal authorities.

DBW: Early on, in the late 1960's and early 1970's, the families of political activists were routinely interviewed and harassed by the various agencies of the state and federal police, to intimidate them and force them to relinquish any support for their relatives. These families were routinely followed by the intelligence units of the various local law enforcement agencies. The police would sit outside their door. The landlords, or the people who they worked for, were routinely approached by the police authorities and told that their employee or tenant was a terrorist, or associated with terrorists, that these individuals were murderers. Oftentimes people were fired from their jobs or evicted from their homes. By the mid-1970's the Black Liberation Movement had been destroyed, so it became increasingly unnecessary for the government to carry out these bold types of surveillance activities. They moved on to develop a more sophisticated program. It's very important to say that, unlike in Europe, in the United States the families of political prisoners do not enjoy the support of a conscious progressive movement. In the United States there are very few organizations on the left that support political prisoners. The families of political prisoners have had to endure the loss of their loved ones alone. In Europe the families of political prisoners have newspapers and newsletters that they put out, they are supported by various organizations. They get to deal with the issue of political repression in an active way.

Q: How about the lawyers?

DBW: The lawyers in the United States have always been subjected to increased surveillance, but again the government tries to mask this under criminal procedures. When George Jackson was assassinated by the state of California, one of his lawyers was accused of participating in the escape attempt, and he had to flee into hiding. He didn't surface until several years later. In the Panther 21 conspiracy case, the law office was broken into, the files stolen, and the law office set on fire. Subsequently we found out that this operation was a so-called government black bag job. A breaking and entering job. They wanted to steal the list of supporters of the Panther 21.

This was in 1970. In the case of other political defendants, some of the lawyers for the American Indian Movement were held in contempt of court for vigorously defending their aims around the issue of the native occupation of Wounded Knee several years ago. In the Brinks case, in 1983, one of the lawyers was cited for contempt for advocating his client's position. Defense teams have been infiltrated by informants— this happened in my case. And the same for the L.A. 8, a Palestinian support group. All throughout the history of last 20 years of political repression, the government has made the defense of political activists an "unprofitable" affair. My defense lawyers had to pay out of their own pocket the expense of defending me and, ultimately, to get me out of prison. And it's the case across the board. Political attorneys, activists' attorneys are shunned by the establishment; they are persecuted by the judges and the legal profession. It's very difficult to defend political cases in the United States.

Q: Would you like to describe the aims and intentions of the Freedom Now campaign with whom you are working?

DBW: I'm currently working with the Campaign to Free Black Political Prisoners and Prisoners-of-War in the United States. We launched this campaign because we realized that Black political prisoners did not have a national campaign, a coordinated effort to raise public awareness as to their plight. We originally worked within the Freedom Now campaign, a coalition of various activists from different movements who saw the necessity for bringing the issue of political repression to the forefront of the American public. We did not feel that organizations such as Amnesty International or Americas Watch were at all concerned with the issue; they were in fact intimidated by the power of the United States government. During the couse of our work, and my travel nationally and internationally for Freedom Now, I realized that it was imperative for the Black community to organize its own efforts around Black political prisoners. Our first objective, of course, is to break through the elaborate fabric of lies weaved by the United States government in the international and national community, which conceals the existence of political prisoners. We have mobilized people across the country on scores of college campuses. We have politicized the issue of political repression in areas not previously reached, mainly among Black trade unions, and gained the support of several of them. The Black and Puerto Rican legislative caucus in New York, which consists of over 30 elected officials, have endorsed our campaign. We have established a regular visitation program for political prisoners in New York and else-where. We are beginning to coordinate the various activities of the political prisoners' defense in regions of the country so that we can raise funds and focus our attention on particular cases at strategic moments. So the Campaign to Free Black Political Prisoners, while very new, is beginning to make headway.

Q: Will you be working in conjunction with the similar support groups in European countries?

DBW: We hope so. We have been in contact with groups in Germany, in Italy and in Spain. We feel that with the collapse of the Soviet Union as a counterweight to U.S. intervention around the world, it is very important that we build an international movement to protect the human rights of people who dissent in the West. And the key is to call for the release of all political prisoners and prisoners-of-war now languishing in the jails of the western democracies.

Q: Can you describe the evidence you have that there is a coordinated policy against political prisoners amongst the western nations?

DBW: In the mid-1980s the United States government established an agency known as the Federal Emergency Management Agency—FEMA—ostensibly to manage national disasters. But FEMA had a much more nefarious political agenda. Its objective was to coordinate the police activities not only among the various states, but also between them and the Federal government. The Joint Anti-Terrorist Task Force was established as a consequence of the counterinsurgency operations carried out against the Black liberation movement and the Puerto Rican nationalist movement. It came into its own in 1978 after the conference in Puerto Rico on the war against international terrorism. At that conference, at which FEMA was represented, the JATTF established a working relationship with the various intelligence agencies in the West, particularly the German BKA, the British M15, the French, Italian and Spanish political police forces. This has gone on from that point until today. We know that some of this coordination was masked, especially in respect to Latin America, under the rubric—again—of the war on drugs. The United States government has provided training for many militarized police forces of these various countries. FEMA has an independent computer system that allows it to penetrate the computer networks of the individual police departments in the U.S., and to transmit information in real time to the other computer link-ups in Europe, Latin America, and Asia. This was best manifested recently by the attempted visit of a group of Black nationalist activists to Libya in 1988. They were denied transit in a European country which was obviously notified by the United States justice department and the JATTF. They were detained during their transit to Libya, although their journey was completely legal. They were debriefed upon their return to the U.S., and any written material that they had was confiscated. The same thing occurred recently with Puerto Rican nationalists in the MLN, the Movimiento de Liberacion Nacional, during a recent tour of Germany a few months ago. They spoke at a number of college campuses and cities in Germany, and upon their arrival in London at Heathrow Airport, all their baggage was confiscated, all their written material taken by the police authorities. Then they were sent on their way. Copies of the confiscated material were subsequently turned over to the U.S. political police. So the coordination between police agencies is as developed as the sharing of military intelligence in the Western alliance.

On Racism, Rap, and Rebellion

Q: What important events since you've been out of prison have shaped the situation of Black people in this country?

Dhoruba Bin Wahad: One of the most significant is the complete dissolution of the Soviet empire. The ramifications of that historical event have yet to be felt and completely absorbed. Let me give you an example: the relationship between the United States government and the African nations has significantly changed. Many of these nations no longer have support from the so-called socialist camp and the communist bloc. As a consequence they have had to negotiate settlements and new relationships with the superpower, the United States, and with the European nations that were on the side of the U.S. in the Cold War.

So with the collapse of the Soviet Union and the end of the Cold War I think there is going to be an increasingly antagonistic development between people of color and the European nation-states. Racism is becoming the foremost tool against people of color immigrating into Europe. The right

Interview conducted by Jim Fletcher in New York City, September 1992.

103

wing is consolidating its political power around laws based on immigration. In the United States, the rise of the racist right and the Aryan Nation and other racist suprematist groups is at an unprecedented high. The ideological underpinning that was there before the advent of the Bolshevik revolution, that is, European racism, is now coming back into the forefront as the cutting edge of progressive struggle. Those movements that do not have an analysis of racism, that do not organize against it, that do not understand its class and economic basis, its basis in state power, these movements will ultimately fail.

Q: Would you say that the struggle against racism is most developed in the United States?

DBW: Yes. We are the only Africans in the diaspora that have lived so closely with white society as such. The colonial experience of the people in the Caribbean or in Africa is different. In these societies Black people were always the majority; the minority, the ruling colonizers, always maintained their aloofness and distance. So although segregation and apartheid in this country was legal and is now *de facto*— it may be illegal but it exists— Black people here have always interacted with the majority culture, and the majority racist power structure, in a profound way. We have influenced and pushed that structure into different directions.

Q: Would you say that the conditions are better here because of that?

DBW: Racism is more effective in Africa and in the Third World precisely because people of color in these places do not really have a handle on the psychosis, or psychological madness of Europeans, especially white Americans. They do not really understand that the United States' ruling elite and the European ruling elite are very sick. They give these people the benefit of the doubt. They will appeal to their humanity and to their pragmatism when in fact both are shot through with irrational delusions of power and racist supremacy. They approach these people as if they were amenable to either democratic sharing of power, the empowerment of people of color, or even recognizing their humanity. The majority of Third World people adopt certain outward manifestations of the civilization, and they see this as progress. Then they come into head-on conflict with the contradiction of that civilization, and they're ill-prepared to deal with it. Black people in the United States have a better understanding of this psychosis. And it's not something that has just begun. It has come out of European history. It's a part of European tribalism, of their genocide of the native peoples, of their ideological and religious fanaticism when they went into Africa, Asia and Latin America.

Q: What kind of effect does that have on people, to become more familiar with madness?

DBW: One of the problems that Black people have in this racist society as a sub-culture—because we have been relegated to a sub-culture in many ways—is separating our own insanity and our own internalized oppression from the madness of the oppressor. Because there's a down side to having lived so close to this oppressor, and that is that we have internalized many of this oppressor's psychoses and madnesses. It plays itself out differently with us because we are powerless to address our own madness in ways that enhance our existence. It's very difficult for Black people to make a clean break with the oppressor because of the proximity in which we live, although Black culture and Black society have always been the dynamic edge to so-called "American culture." Black culture has always given it its vitality and has informed everything from the style of clothes to the language, to art, to social relationships.

Q: Do you think that in a Third World situation there's a possibility of making a cleaner kind of progress?

DBW: I think with the collapse of the Soviet Union there's a possibility now for the first time of establishing a serious international movement of people of color and poor people, a movement that is directed against the hegemony of the European nation-states. Now the contradictions can be developed in a much clearer fashion, the contradiction between North and South, between Europeans and people of color. We have seen the beginnings of that type of movement in the radical left within Europe. How it will manifest itself in each country is a different question.

Q: The movement against racism in Europe seems qualitatively different from the way the problem comes out here.

DBW: A lot of things that happened here twenty years ago are just beginning to happen in Europe. Widespread homelessness for instance is beginning to be seen in Paris and Germany and England, and the homeless are increasingly people of color. People of color have always been segregated into ghettos, but now these ghettos are even further marginalized. In France people of color tend to live in the suburbs, and these suburbs have the worst transportation, the worst housing, the worst public services. People view these suburbs as ghettos. There are differences of course, but the youth in these ghettos suffer the same problems as the youth in our communities. They are harrassed, they are brutalized and murdered by the police, their families are on the dole, on state welfare, they are subject to a whole panoply of rules and regulations designed to dehumanize them. Crack is coming into Europe now, and it's mainly coming into the poorer communities. So a lot of the things that we see happening here are beginning to happen in Europe, and what that may tell us is that Western civilization, given its contradictions, shares a certain fundamental ideology and a fundamental hierarchy of power, and that revolves around caste, class and gender. People of color are going to prison at an increasing rate. The states in Europe are forced to build larger prisons at the same time that they're moving towards federation and breaking down the borders and the legal barriers between peoples in Europe. This new openness does not really include people of color.

Q: When the Los Angeles rebellions happened after the Rodney King verdict, I saw a guy from Germany interviewed on TV. He was walking around L.A., in all the rubble, and the only thing he said into the camera was "This is crazy, the United States hates Black people." Was that a naive statement on his part?

DBW: I don't think that at its root the racism is any different. Up until several years ago Germany didn't have a significant population of Black people; the people of color they did have tended to come for economic reasons and tried to blend in as much as possible. The contradiction between Germans themselves is rife with tribalism, just between the Germans themselves. Racism against people of color there is just beginning to raise its ugly head now that they have this influx of people of color. The Germans have not had to deal with an internal colony and massive presence of Black people.

Q: Do you think that a European, in order to understand racism, has to go through the madness of experiencing it as a racist himself?

DBW: The only way for a European or any white person to understand racism is through the interaction with people of color in a principled way, through dealing with people of color in the struggle against white-skin privilege.

Q: When the riots, or rebellions, were happening in L.A., did you feel that big changes were taking place?

DBW: The rebellion in L.A. was very important because it sent a signal. People had taken Black people for granted to such a degree that they believed that they could do anything to us, they could perpetrate any type of injustice, any type of indignity, and we wouldn't react, we wouldn't do anything, we wouldn't struggle against it. The L.A. rebellion showed that there is a deep-seated rage against this racist system shared by a very large segment of the Black community, and that absent a movement, this rage and this hatred for the system will not find any particular type of political expression. It will express itself in nihilistic behavior.

Q: Do you look at what happened there as nihilistic?

DBW: No, I look at it as a reaction to a gross injustice that Black people felt. At the same time, without a movement to inform this type of sentiment, this legitimate feeling, and harness and direct it, the rebellion soon peters out and charla-

108

tans and opportunists come forward to misdirect any follow-up.

Q: Some people say that the uprising in L.A. was a multi-racial thing.

DBW: Oh definitely. It was a reaction against a state that has marginalized people of color and poor people, and that has brutalized young people in ways that we can hardly imagine. The life of a young person growing up in this society today, especially a Black person or a Chicano or Latino youth, is a very frightful experience. And the powerlessness of our communities only enhances the desperation and the nihilism of our youth. When people have nothing to fight for, they begin to self-destruct. The absence of a movement has made Black youth unable to process their alienation in a way that could benefit their community. The rebellion in L.A. did transcend color-lines because alienation in this society is acutely felt by young people. This society is impersonal. It's a youth culture but it doesn't value youth. It exploits them, it destroys them, it snatches their humanity from them. In order to survive young people have developed lifestyles and ideologies to deal with that. The rebellion had to do with alienation across the board, between young and poor people and the status quo. This is why we saw young white people blowing into various stores, why young Asians and Blacks and Latinos were together in the streets in L.A.

Q: Rap music is sometimes presented as a kind of movement, or the closest thing to a revolutionary force...

DBW: The culture that evolves from the underclass has

the potential to speak to the underclass in ways that other cultural forms cannot. Rap music came up from young people on the streets who were marginalized— by the music, by the culture, who had no places to go, and who needed to hear music that reflected their reality and spoke to them. So rap music in a sense has the potential, like all other art forms, to serve a revolutionary purpose, but it doesn't mean that in and of itself it's revolutionary. There are some people who try to say that rap music is revolutionary in and of itself. I would have disagreement with that. The message is not always revolutionary, and the use of the idiom of the voice over a bass and drums is something that has always been part of Black African culture in one form or another, so I don't see how it's revolutionary even in terms of its artistic expression. But it does have the potential to be revolutionary. If we develop a liberation movement in this country that speaks to the needs of Black people, one of the ways that we can communicate is through cultural forms. But you have to have a movement... Rap music in my view is not necessarily progressive. It depends on the context in which the music is played, it depends on the message that the music is giving up, and it depends on whether the masses of people are organized in a way in which these cultural forms express their struggle.

Q: Is an effective movement always a very deliberate organization, or is it sometimes some kind of unimaginable happening that occurred just because forces came together that way?

DBW: If you examine other movements you'll see that although the conditions had to be right for revolutionary change to occur, the process of ripening those conditions in a progressive way, in a way that harnessed people's potential and energy in a way that empowered them, had come about as a consequence of an organized movement, and movements must be organized by elements who share a certain vision, a concept of what they're fighting for, why they're fighting for it, who the enemy is and why they're the enemy, why it's necessary to fight and how we get from point A to point B. The leading element in any movement should be those with the most progressive politics.

Q: I've heard several times that by the year 2020 white people will no longer be a majority in the United States. Do you see potential for a serious change in the face of the United States?

DBW: Given that type of demographics, of course there will be some changes and maybe some significant changes, but I think that what we're witnessing now is the depoliticization of racism, the watering down of racism. I mean up until L.A. the issue of race and racism was not high on the national agenda. If you asked people what were the most important problems confronting the United States, racism wouldn't have been amongst the top four, but it is today, as a consequence of L.A.

The U.S. may become less and less a white male preserve, but it doesn't mean that white males won't continue to control society. But they will have to control society in a different way, or they will have to apply a different twist, a different spin on the ideology of racism. We see that through the appointment of Clarence Thomas, through Colin Powell's position on the Joint Chiefs of Staff, through the promotion of various Black police chiefs to head police agencies.The institutions that these negroes have risen to the forefront of are institutions that still carry out racist policies. The police still

111

brutalize and murder Black people under Black police chiefs. The cities still fail to provide goods and services to the majority of people of color and poor working people in those cities under Black mayors. The United States Army has gone into Panama, it has gone into Kuwait and Iraq under a Black chairman of the Joint Chiefs of Staff. The Supreme Court has carried out some of its most reactionary decisions with the inclusion of a woman and a Black judge in the Supreme Court. So if women are coming into positions of prominence, and if Black people are becoming a majority in this country, it doesn't necessarily mean that the real relationships of power in this country are also changing over, or going into the hands of women and Black people. What it means is that those who control power have to do so in a different way. Racism is a phenomenon that readily adapts to change in circumstances and conditions and can maintain its influence and its control over people in subtle ways. And the culture reinforces these things. This is why we are told today in the media that Arabs are the enemy—they're usually defined as fundamentalists and terrorists—and that Black people are the enemy—they're usually defined as perpetrators of crime and drug dealers or people who are crazy on crack, or crazy because they're homeless—or Latinos, who are drug dealers and drug cowboys. All of these stereotypes have created new racist symbols, but at the same time they have not used the old racist language. They send the same signals but they use a different language. So when we see a Latino is driving a new car and he's wearing a silk suit and his Versace silk shirt, we immediately believe that he's a Latin American drug dealer or someone so involved, and that's racist. This racism is subtly concealed by the media and used to manipulate people's opinions.

112

Q: What's your interpretation of what happened in New York City's Washington Heights neighborhood?

DBW: You mean the murder of José Garcia? Well we have said for a long time that the police do not treat people of color and poor people the same way they treat rich white people. The majority of policemen see the poor communities as a jungle in which they have to be the number one predator, the most feared animal in the jungle, and they carry out this absurd analysis to its logical conclusion and that's treating people of color as if their lives were insignificant. We've also said that in the Black community the police have played a heavy role in the importation and distribution of drugs. I don't know the particulars of this dude Officer O'Keefe but it's been reported that he's had a relationship with this policeman Dowd who's recently been indicted for trafficking drugs and acting as an enforcer for a drug ring. But more importantly, the treatment of Dominicans is no different from the treatment of any people of color in this city. The police have murdered people from all these communities with impunity. I think the difference is that the Dominicans don't have the same long track record that we have in terms of struggling against power in this country and therefore they have not mobilized themselves in order to deal with police brutality in this country. But I think that's changing.

Q: Do you have anything to say about Brooklyn's Crown Heights, where Blacks and Hasidic Jews are fighting? Do you think it's more puzzling or more complicated than the typical racial situation?

DBW: No, I think it's a typical situation in which people who have enjoyed white-skin privilege have a certain relationship with the police. The police protect them, they look out for them, they're on the payroll, so to speak, of these communities, I'm talking about the Hasidic community. The Hasidic community has never come out and opposed racist attacks on Black people, they have never come out and protested against police brutality in the Black community. They identify with certain factors of this society's culture and political structure that serve them, and one of the factors that serve them of course is that they're white. But also they are very shrewd in the way they have organized themselves and used their community to its maximum in terms of political clout. If Black people had organized themselves the way the Jews in Crown Heights did, we would be viewed as a threat to the system and we would be attacked and vilified and criminalized.

Q: If you did organize yourselves that way, would you be a threat to the system?

DBW: Sure.

Q: So it's true, that's a valid judgement...

DBW: Black people and people of color and women will always be a threat to the system whenever they organize to empower themselves because the system is partly based on their disempowerment.

Mumia Abu-Jamal

... Herman Bell

Hanif Shabazz Bey

Dhoruba Bin Wahad (released)

George Brown (in exile)

Mark Cook

Donald Cox (in exile)

Malik El-Amin

Eddie Ellis (on parole)

Chui Ferguson (on parole)

Herman Ferguson (on parole)

Bashir Hameed

Abdul Haqq

Robert Seth Hayes

Teddy (Jah) Heath

Charles Lee Herron

Mohaman Koti

Richard Mafundi Lake ...

Interview from Death Row

MAJ: My name is Mumia Abu-Jamal. I'm on death row in Pennsylvania. I'm a member and a long-time supporter of the MOVE organization and ex-president of Black Journalists in Philadelphia. I'm still continuing revolutionary journalism. I'm fighting my conviction, fighting the sentence, fighting for my life, and fighting to create revolution in America.

Q: How did you meet MOVE in the first place?

MAJ: I met MOVE while covering them in Philadelphia. No one who was in Philadelphia from the seventies to the mid-eighties, can claim not to know about MOVE. MOVE members have been active and above-ground in Philadelphia since 1973. I've been reading in magazines a lot about the animal liberation movement. In 1973 they were in the Philadelphia Zoo protesting caged exploitation of animals, and they were beaten for it, they were jailed for it, and they got ridiculously high bails for it. When I first heard about MOVE people eating garlic, the women having babies with no mid-wife, no drugs, no medication, no husband, just themselves and their God-given instinct for motherhood, when I

Interview conducted late in 1989 at Huntingdon Prison in Pennsylvania.

117

first heard about MOVE people being beaten for protesting Frank Rizzo or protesting at the zoo against the encagement of animals, I thought they were crazy. But more and more, you hear people embracing those same kinds of ideas. Now you have an Animal Liberation Front where people are doing the same types of things that MOVE was doing ten, fifteen years ago, but it ain't crazy all of a sudden. Now you have people saying, "Eat garlic, it's good for you, it'll help your heart rate and clean your body out." Before, they said MOVE smelled like a bunch of pizzas. All the things that I've seen, instead of being incredible are very credible, instead of radical are very natural, are very do-able.

What MOVE represents is an idea that people can move away from the system and use the principle of life to survive. They've been through every jail in Philadelphia, they've been beaten in every police district, largely in Black West Philadelphia, for standing up for their belief in defending life. So as reporter covering them I became exposed to them, as opposed to reading about them, and found out that what I read about them had no relationship to the kind of people they were and what they were about. Every published report was tinged with prejudice and hatred. Its only function was to give a revolting, distancing picture of MOVE. Say a member of MOVE, Ramona Africa or Debbie Africa, would make a statement, they wouldn't say what those words were, they would say it was "full of rhetoric." It's considered unfair to look at what America says about constitutional rights and call that rhetoric. But when MOVE people talk about the brutality, the injustice they have seen in these courtrooms in America, and they give examples, documented examples, that's called "rhetoric."

Q: What do you think was the threat that MOVE represented?

MAJ: The idea. There's nothing more powerful than an idea. MOVE is a family of revolutionaries, committed to resisting the system. MOVE believes that this entire reform world-system is a threat to life, and needs to be confronted, and they'll begin to resist it, by any means necessary.

Q: And that would include armed struggle?

MAJ: That means *any* means necessary. Many people will recall Malcolm X used those words. If Malcolm meant what he said, then it shouldn't be remarkable for people to follow that dictum. "By any means necessary" means any necessary means to achieve a revolutionary result. And MOVE will use any means necessary.

Q: When you say revolutionary, what do you mean?

MAJ: Revolution means change. It means total change. One of the things that people think of when they hear "revolution" is perhaps a Marxist revolution based on Marxist–Leninist principles and economic transformation in the means of production. We don't consider that a total revolution. MOVE is not Marxist–Leninist, does not present an economic solution to the plagues which burden society. The challenge is the complete system. Today when you look at what's happening in Eastern Europe, the Marxists must be pulling their hair out by the roots because all of the theories of how revolution is supposed to occur are completely upside-down. What's happening is you're getting resistance from the masses to a presumably revolutionary government, but it's a government that's just as corrupt, just as brutal in terms of their secret service, just as underground and as filthy as the capitalist's police services and the capitalist politicians. When you look at the savage brutality inflicted on the poor and the people by the police and by the system of the United States, you can see a mirror image of that same reality in Eastern Europe today. If people were satisfied in Eastern Europe, they wouldn't be clamoring to tear down the walls. The economic interpretation of history and life is not holistic enough. It doesn't cover the whole globe, it doesn't cover the full personality of people. You can find corruption, oppression, everywhere on the earth. I would love to see somebody from Danzig or Gdansk, or Leipzig, come to Times Square and see people homeless. As many as 3.5 million people in America are homeless. They don't believe it, they don't really understand what America is. Those people in Eastern Europe are under brutal state-police terror, but they have a barrier of safety for housing and food. It ain't the best, but it's a whole lot better than being homeless and living in a cardboard box like three million American men, women and kids. We're caught up in a rat-race that has no good end.

I think that this age in society is a pivotal one. Clearly, it's not working. Clearly, what's been happening in Eastern Europe is not working. I would like to tell those people that this ain't gonna solve your problems either. The homelessness, it's not gonna be solved by embracing this capitalist dollar. There's got to be some middle ground, some middle range, where people can be free. So MOVE's revolution is against external government, any force that inflicts its will on people's will to be free. Because the will to be free is in-born. It's innate. It's in all humanity, all of life. That's the teaching of John Africa.

Q: I'm interested in the collective assumption of the surname "Africa."

MAJ: MOVE members take the name *Africa* as a form of respect for the founder of the MOVE organization, who was John Africa. We recognize that all human life began in Africa, the first man, child, woman, to walk on earth, walked, trod, played, lived in Africa.

Q: The "mainstream Left," whoever that is, has not really paid much attention or given much support either to MOVE or to your case, or to a group that's definitely been under siege.

MAJ: Absolutely. I think the "Left" in America has been intimidated by the Reagan Right. You've had eight years of Reagan really setting the agenda, of Reagan setting the tone in America for what will be permissible and what will not. When you consider that the bombing of May 13th, 1985 happened under a Democratic mayor, a presumably Left mayor, Philadelphia's first Black mayor, than there are more blurs in that whole Left–Right dichotomy. It doesn't work.

Q: Your career as a journalist began about the time you were covering MOVE?

MAJ: No, it was earlier than that. My career as a journalist began with the Black Panther newspaper in Philadelphia, with York, the Ministry of Information and on the Black Panther newspaper in Berkeley, California. There is where I learned how to write from a revolutionary perspective. In fact, I got into broadcasting because I enjoyed writing so well, and not because I enjoyed broadcasting. That's the background for me. It isn't school, because I flunked out of all the schools I went to.

Q: You were pretty young when you joined the Black Panthers. How did it happen?

MAJ: I was beaten into the Black Panther Party. As a youth in the sixties I was impressed by the Black Power Movement that was sweeping Black America and the Black world, in Africa and the Caribbean. So, I remember, me and a brother named Eddie Jones and a few other brothers, we went to a demonstration in South Philadelphia, Philadelphia Spectrum, a big sporting arena. This was 1968 and George Wallace III, I think that's his name, was running for President under the American Independent Party. In retrospect it was kind of crazy to think that we would go down to a demonstration in South Philadelphia, which is predominantly white, and protest against George Wallace coming to Philadelphia. But at that time we believed that it was our city as well. So we did it. And every one of us got our asses kicked by the plainclothes policemen. You've probably heard the tale, "I'll beat you so bad your own Mama won't know you." Well, it has particular relevance to me because as I was laying in the Hospital, charged with assault, and aggravated assault and beating of a police officer, my own mother walked by me, looked me dead in the eyes and kept walking because she couldn't recognize me. I was beaten unrecognizable. I was in my mid-teens at that time. From that period, and from those experiences, from me having to go through the hell of that, and seeing the complete lack of power of people to resist that, I was attracted to the Black Panther Party, plus stuff I was reading, *Ramparts Magazine*, which turned me on to other radical materials to read. So because there was not a functioning, active Black Panther Party at that time in Philadelphia, we founded one and built it. I was their Lieutenant of Information. My function was really propaganda, putting out information in support of the party, and about the political situation in Philadelphia, so I like to say I was beaten to the Black Panther Party. But I was seduced into the MOVE organization by the loveliness of its members.

Q: What was the climate of the city at that time?

MAJ: It could be called politically charged because at that time, in late 1981, nine members of the MOVE organization had just been sentenced to thirty to a hundred years for a crime that everybody knew they did not commit. Nine people cannot kill one man. You also had the arrest of other MOVE members up in Rochester, New York, their extradition to Philadelphia, and their subsequent conviction. What you had in Philadelphia in 1981 was the naked state terrorism of the Philadelphia judiciary against the MOVE organization. It was like, "Let's wipe them out." It's impossible for me to say what my feelings were at that time, sitting in a courtroom, seeing that kind of naked injustice. It rankled me to the core. I said a minute ago that I was introduced into the MOVE organization by the loveliness and goodness of its people. I was probably enraged as well. Sitting in a trial, in an official capacity, objective as a journalist, and seeing that the law really didn't matter, that it didn't matter whether a man was considered guilty, it didn't matter what the law says your rights were. I read a quote a few days ago, by Thomas Jefferson, that says, "I have no right which another can take away from me." I think about that quote very often because in the MOVE organization all the rights that are supposedly guaranteed to our people, the right to self-representation, the right to defend yourself in your trial, were summarily stripped and denied.

Never in my wildest dreams would I ever think that it

would happen to me. You always say, "Well, it happens to the other fellow." But when I was on trial, and I exercised the purely constitutional right to defend myself, it was denied. It went through me like a thunderbolt. "It can happen," I realized, "it is happening." And it happens every day. People can talk about rights 'til the cows come home. But when people try to exercise those rights, they find that those rights were not rights after all. They're platitudes put out there by the government to have people think that they are free.

From the very beginning of the trial, I intended to select my own jury. Jury selection, called "voir dire," means that you can talk to the jury, get a feel for how they feel about legal ideals. Every lawyer does it every day. It's a very important part of the trial, in fact I believe that it's the core of the trial. The district attorney said that I "terrorized" one juror. And the judge said, "He's stripped," and put the lawyer in the position. I didn't want the lawyer to do it, I wanted to do it because the lawyer's life wasn't at stake. But I had to sit there silently and let another guy do that, who really didn't want to do it as well. I was reading about that in some of the law books and it seems as if one of the first acts that the revolutionary world knew—the United States Congress enacted it around 1780, signed by George Washington, the first President— was the right of a person to defend himself in his criminal trial. It can be 200, 300 years old and it's meaningless. Because if you can't exercise it, it's not a right. Everywhere I turn, when I try to defend myself, it's like: "Shut up, sit up or you're gonna be kicked outta here," or "you're gonna get bound and gagged." In fact I was kicked out of the courtroom almost every day because I felt that strongly about that principle.

Q: So, in this trial you were convicted. What were the charges?

MAJ: I was charged with homicide of a police officer in Philadelphia. I was convicted of murder in the first degree and sentenced to death and two and a half to five. I'm presently appealing.

Q: I know you can't talk about some things because you have a pending appeal.

MAJ: That's true. I was sentenced to death by the court of common pleas of Philadelphia in July of 1983. I appealed to the Pennsylvania Supreme Court which is the only court you can appeal to from a sentence of death. That appeal was denied in May of 1989, but it's on re-argument, so it's still pending before that court at this time.

Q: Was the death penalty the jury's recommendation or was that the judge's decision?

MAJ: In Pennsylvania it's the jury's recommendation. It cannot be overridden by the judge. One of the things that links my background with the MOVE organization and with the Black Panther Party is that in the sentencing phase of the trial the prosecutor introduced an article from the *Philadelphia Enquirer,* an interview with me when I was a young teen and Lieutenant of Information of the Black Panther Party. He cross-examined me on that article. What you had was the sudden introduction of the Black Panther Party into a case in which it didn't fit. The political nature is evident. If the jury were not predominantly white, middle-class, older, in their fifties; if they were young people, Blacks, Puerto Ricans, who

125

had knowledge of the current contemporary history of Philadelphia, "Black Panther" would have had a different kind of impact. The words "Black Panther" mean different things depending on peoples' perspective, their history, their political orientation. There is a generation in America for whom the Black Panthers were not a threat but a lift, a sign of hope for a time. For another generation and class in America the Black Panthers were a threat. The prosecutor knew that exceedingly well, because that was used to bring back the death penalty. When it hit the jury it was like a bolt of electricity.

Q: Would you consider yourself a political prisoner?

MAJ: Most people, if not all people, are imprisoned for a political reason. For a political effect. Prisons in America are political organs of the state. When you have people who resist the government and the system, then you have people who are imprisoned and in a cage for their political beliefs. Yes, I am a political prisoner. As a matter of fact I believe every prisoner in America is a political prisoner. That might be too radical, that might not be accepted by the United Nations, but that's my position.

Q: Are you saying that all prisoners are political prisoners because crime is caused by poverty and social reasons?

MAJ: Absolutely. But not just that. What I was thinking is that every prosecution is a public and symbolic act, a political act by the state to give the populace an illusion of control, to show that "we're taking care of this problem." When you point to corruption in a politician or a policeman, what you have is the policeman losing his job, or the politician losing his pension, but you don't have the same kind of punishment. It's a different effect. Recently in Philadelphia you had one of the biggest cases of judicial corruption in America. It rivaled the Greylord Scandal in Chicago, Illinois. You had about thirteen civic judges of the courts of common pleas in Philadelphia charged with taking money in a roofer scandal for full favors. Several of those judges were convicted, but most of them were not. Most of them were not even prosecuted. They were brought before the board of the Supreme Court of Pennsylvania, charged with violating the ethics code, and made to resign. Many of them are still working attorneys in Philadelphia. You can be too corrupt to be a judge, but just corrupt enough to be a lawyer.

Q: How do you explain the bombing of MOVE headquarters on May 13, 1985?

MAJ: One would have to look very long and hard to find an example even remotely close to the bombing of MOVE people on May 13th, 1985 in America. I've heard people say that the bombing in Tulsa, Oklahoma in the 1920s was similar, but Tulsa represented the culmination of a race riot. You didn't have purely state forces at work against a Black community or a Black family. You had so-called private white folks with guns and cars. And you had cops and you had troops. May 13th, 1985 was a state operation from the very beginning. If someone were to read what was written about May 13th, they might come away with the opinion that it was a blunder, a badly failed operation, or that's the impression that they would like you to have. In fact it was deeply planned at least a year in advance, and they achieved a lot of their objectives. You don't attempt to evict people from their own homes with dynamite. You don't evacuate the whole neighborhood at seven o'clock in the morning if all you want is an eviction. In police raids of Black Panther headquarters, in Los Angeles, in Philadelphia, in New York and other places, they never evacuated neighborhoods—they just made their moves. This was a pre-meditated attempt to liquidate the MOVE organization.

Q: What was their argument?

MAJ: Civil eviction. The home was owned by a MOVE person. They said MOVE was making too much noise with a bullhorn. MOVE does use bullhorns. MOVE speaks clearly, loudly, its beliefs, our beliefs, the teaching of John Africa about this system, about the corruption, about the injustice in this country and the history of MOVE people. The problem with that argument though, is that for about three weeks before May 13th the bullhorn wasn't operable. It was broken. So that noise argument doesn't fit. There can be no approximate reason for May 13th, other than the apparent one. May 13th, 1985 was pre-planned, staged by the local, state and federal government, with one aim in mind: to wipe out MOVE forever, to silence MOVE's voice so that no one could ever hear that radical spirit being expressed anymore.

Q: Thinking historically of your involvment with the Panthers and then with MOVE, do you think there is an FBI strategy, or a law enforcement strategy against both the Panthers in the sixties and seventies and then against MOVE in the eighties? Is "terrorism" the new buzzword of law enforcement?

MAJ: Terrorism is a new buzzword, but underlining that is the ability of the state's media to label "terrorist" anything that they see as threatening and by that labeling isolate that person, that group, that organization, those people, and put them beyond the pale, so that whatever happens to them is cool. Edward S. Herman called that *The Real Terror Network.* What he uncovered is that the PLO and the other groups that are maligned and slurred as terrorists in the media, they're really small fry, retail terrorists. Wholesale terroristm is conducted by the United States government, which arms the government in El Salvador so that they can have helicopter gunships come in poor neighborhoods and bomb the FMLN. But in the *New York Times,* it's the FMLN that is described as a terrorist organization, not the Cristiani government, or Roberto D'Aubuisson, who tortured people with blow-torches and was called by Pat Robinson "a pretty nice fella." Terrorism is a label used by the system so that people don't have to find out what's really happening. The *Philadelphia Enquirer* recently made a very slick, quick reference to the MOVE organization as a terrorist organization. One of my sisters, Ramona Africa, had a brilliant reply. She explained that calling MOVE terrorist is to find no meaning in the word. It was the Philadelphia police department, the state government of Pennsylvania, the FBI, the ATF of the U.S. government who bombed MOVE people on May 13th, 1985. But no one would call any of those organizations or their employer— the U.S. government—terrorist. But why weren't they? They created mass murder in a major city in America. And not one of them had ever been charged with any crime at all. Only Ramona Africa—guilty only of survival—is in jail following May 13th, 1985. She's been in jail for almost six years. The Philadelphia police department preplanned, for months, the detonation of the MOVE headquarters. They mixed chemicals, they got all kinds of explosives. One of the explosives was used in the Claymore mines in Vietnam—Totex, I think it was. The Philadelphia police department got these chemicals from the Alcohol, Tobacco and Firearms Department of the U.S. Treasury. FBI agents slipped it to them, they built this bomb, they dropped it on MOVE, and nobody goes to jail except Ramona Africa. She's the only one charged with a crime, the only one convicted.

Q: How many people died in that bombing?

MAJ: At least eleven people from MOVE. All the life in that house was related, so cats, dogs, all our relatives, our brothers, our family. According to published reports, at least eleven but no one knows because they reduced that place to ashes. They destroyed and dismembered people. It's very easy for a journalist like the *Philadelphia Enquirer* reporter to just say: "MOVE, you know, the terrorist group..." But no one says: "FBI, the terrorist group," even when there are documented cases of terrorism, even over and above what they did to the MOVE organization. The COINTELPRO program was a terroristic program. Its function was to terrorize radicals, revolutionaries, opponents of government programs, to stigmatize and isolate them from the general population. They sent letters, smut letters, from husbands to wives. They sent letters to employers. They sent letters from one radical organization to another, to try to incite violence between those organizations. In the Black Panther Party, out in L.A.—I think it was in 1969—a brother was killed because there were letters going between organizations that were not authored by Panthers, they were authored by FBI agents in some dark office in California to incite hatred and division between radical groups. So who's the terrorist?

Q: So the movement from COINTELPRO, for instance,

to the bombing of the MOVE headquarters, shows a change in referent, even though it might be a continuation of strategy?

MAJ: I would think it was an escalation rather than a change. A change in degree. COINTELPRO was underground, unseen government action. May 13th, 1985 was an overt government attempt to destroy, wipe out, totally eliminate the MOVE organization. In all the years that I was a Panther and before that, make no mistake, the government tried, very viciously, to wipe out the Black Panther Party. The point is, they never went to those kinds of lengths. In 1972, when the LAPD staged a raid on the Black Panther officers in Los Angeles on Central Avenue, they tried to kill Panthers. They shot, they sent grenades, they bombed, they did all that stuff, but they didn't do the kind of stuff that they did in 1985. The Iron Curtain and the Berlin Wall fell down. But in the United States more walls are going up, more prisons growing up, more repression. America looks hypocritically over the Warsaw Block and talks about the rights of people, but in the meantime they're taking more rights, day after day, from Americans in America. A right that cannot be exercised is no right at all.

Q: What do you think has permitted the escalation?

MAJ: Politics. A kind of American *glasnost* is opening because you don't have a Soviet threat anymore. The whole Communist bogeyman is gone. Because the national security state no longer has an external threat, they develop an internal threat. The watchword for the 1990s is drugs and revolutionaries, radicals. They don't mean Soviet communists, although they might mean American communists. They mean people in Central America, like Nicaraguans and the Salvadoreans; they mean people in North America, like the resistance conspiracy defendants, like MOVE members; they mean anyone who intends to resist the Empire. Anyone who stands up against a political system and says "This ain't right, we're not going along with this." Drugs, again, is now used as the banner for a new war, a new war that America has created. When you talk about Nicaragua, Central America, you can't ignore the history of America bringing it home to the whole drug problem. You have arms merchants flying to Honduras and Costa Rica, to air force bases, dropping off arms for the contras, loading up on cocaine, flying back to the United States, landing in U.S. Air Force bases, and walking away like nothing was wrong with that. So when I hear these politicians talk about "Just Say No," they never said no to the people bringing cocaine here using U.S. Air Force bases; everything was alright. It's only when that got reported in the foreign press that people said, "Oh, yeah, let's investigate that."

Q: It was brought up at the Iran Contra hearings and no one picked it up. The politicians just looked the other way.

MAJ: I just read that report by the Sub-committee on Drugs, Law Enforcement and Terrorism headed by Congressman Kerry from Massachusetts, and it's right in there. You can write to your congressman and get a 100-page report which shows how the U.S. Government imported drugs in the United States, and it's like, "Next!" Or "I got an election coming up, we'll get back to that." It's nothing. No problem. This is not to say that drugs are not a very serious problem in Black America, in Spanish America, in America period. You've got drugs decimating generations in America. Wiping out their minds, their soul, their bodies, their futures. I think the U.S. Government is the biggest drug pusher of all. If you were to compare a profile of the primary drug user in America, it wouldn't be a Black kid in North Philadelphia or in Harlem, it'd be a forty-year-old white male, who has the financial resources to go after cocaine. It's more palatable, politically, to kick in the doors of a Black family in North Philadelphia, to use a battering ram in L.A. to knock down the wall of a family in Los Angeles—a Black family or a Spanish family—because they're less politically connected; there's less political repercussion for those acts of police violence. America, because of its origins and because of its economic need, must have some war to fight.

Q: Initially terrorists were seen as agents of the Evil Empire, now that has shifted and it's becoming much more of a North–South, rich country–poor country issue.

MAJ: Absolutely, because this empire cannot survive without its external markets. Reagan said with a straight face that the Contras are the moral equivalent of our founding fathers. Either he's saying a very good truth about the degeneracy of the founding fathers, or he's lost in a fog. I mean these guys were ex-members of the National Guard, rapists, thieves, killers. But they are the moral equivalent of our founding fathers. I guess from an American Indian perspective and an African perspective, perhaps they are.

Q: Sometimes those who are often subject to attacks by the system don't receive them as that. Why are people lulled or beaten into submission?

MAJ: I think it's the power of apathy. What you have here in America is pull this lever every three years, every four years, for a politician, and that's perceived as politics. That's political action. Well, nothing could be further from the truth. True political action is learning about the world around you, or teaching others about the world around you, on a daily basis, because everything has a poltical interaction. When people talk about democracy, I kind of sneer a little bit. I was reading a book on philosophy and it gave me a breakdown on Athens at the time of Plato. You had four hundred thousand residents of Athens, two hundred and fifty thousand of them slaves. That's not democracy, that's slave-ocracy. People in the Soviet Union had bureacracy, state capitalism. You can talk about democracy all you want, but the United States clearly doesn't give a damn about democracy. In South Africa they support the minority government. They cleary don't give a damn about democracy in Nicaragua, about democracy in El Salvador, or anywhere peoples' interests threaten capital. In Nicaragua capitalist-armed contra-revolutionaries enter the country from foreign bases, supported, armed by America, to kill, destroy the infrastructure of Nicaragua. Democracy? What if someone did that in United States? If Nicaragua sponsored three-hundred-thousand counter-revolutionaries, or whatever, to come into the United States, there would be a bit of problem, wouldn't you say? Democracy is a watchword that's used for a catch-all phrase: democratic people are suspposedly those people that America supports. Well then why did America support Pinochet's coup in Chile, when a democratically elected president, Allende—who happened to be a socialist—was elected? Why did they bomb his palace and destroy his government, and install a government that they wanted? Democracy? It's a word, it's a label that they throw on people, like "terrorist," because they control the media.

What you have now, more than any other time in America's history, is more corporate, multi-national control of the media. In Philadelphia, newspapers are all owned by the same corporate entity. They say they have separate editorial departments, but if you have one owner, let's be realistic, you can only please one owner. So when the media gives a certain slant, it's always pro-government. The government is right, they don't do anything wrong. The only times newspapers really get investigative is if dealing with someone else's sexual foibles, instead of a real, basic, economic, social, political breakdown on what's happening in America. I am a print journalist, but I spent much of my "professional life" as a broadcast journalist because any recognition of the consuming habits of Americans today indicates that literacy is dying. People would much more easily flick the switch and turn on the tube than read a paper. It's far too easy to just get your information that way. If that's the way it's gonna be, that's the way it's gonna be. That's the way it is. But the reality is that there's a kind of autonomy in writing and in printed works that television doesn't address. Maybe I'm biased because I like reading so much. But I get the feeling that reading the unedited version of *To Die for the People* by Huey Newton or Inguji Watiango's *Barrel of a Pen,* or the philosophies and opinions of Marcus Garvey, or Malcolm X's stories and his autobiography, is immensely more informative, in terms of its depth, than a thirty-minute mini-drama on NBC—which really is 22 minutes when you take out the commercials and which subtracts all the controversial stuff, because "We don't want to defend this group over here...."

It's like the media is the message, and in the form of media that is prevailing today, the message is determined by who pays the bills—the advertiser. They really determine what lives and what doesn't. What gets aired and what doesn't. The problem is that the all-powerful element in that form of media is the editor. Not even the reporter or the producer. It's the editor who determines how a certain story is slanted and how it gets cut down and used. I worked for a major Philadelphia radio station and back during the May 20th confrontation of MOVE, in Center City Philadelphia, I'd hop on my twelve-speed, ride up to the village, get a few bites, talk to the family to see if there was anything newsworthy and go back. A news director called me one night and said, "Listen, man, I heard this story, you and Chuckie Africa, Jesus Christ, Mumia, that's not news." And from his perspective, it wasn't. It was a dead story. But several weeks after he said that August 8th exploded, and it was news all over the world. It was broadcast in Argentina, in Africa. A brother in Germany saw it on TV, the beating of Delbert Africa. So what we determine is news as reporters is not really important, it's what the editors allow, and what the advertisers, in the final analysis, allow. I remember one program director at a talk station I used to work for who forbade me from mentioning MOVE on the air. "If you say MOVE once more," he said, "you're going to get fired!" I quit. (*Laughs.*) But it's reality. Those people determine what the news is. And perhaps if the Africans were allowed a fair forum to speak about the abuses of MOVE history and MOVE life, maybe May 13th, maybe August 18th, would not have happened. It would not have been necessary. When I first read some numbers—I was anticipating this interview—I realized that there are 30.1 million people in poverty in America and my first reaction was "Damn! There's 30 million Black people in America." But of course, that's not the percentage. There are millions of whites in poverty, millions of Spanish in poverty, of all people in America, of all races. But you would not believe that if you were to look at the "Cosby Show," which is getting bonkers numbers, not just in the U.S. but in South Africa. They have no problem with the "Cosby Show" in South Africa. It promotes the ideal of a middle class in a country badly in need of a middle class to buffer the apartheid regime. It promotes the possibility of a better tomorrow for people who have such a miserable today in America and around the world. It's very easy for the "Cosby Show" to get billions in advertising and stuff like that because the "Cosby Show" is not the reality in Black America. It's a reflection of an ideal that is so far from the real as to be, you know, comic.

I don't have much respect for media. As a journalist it might be damning to say that. I really don't, because we become the prostitutes of the medium that we embrace. I've seen that with people that have entered the business with me, who now, because of their personal and "professional ambition and growth," cannot relate to the kind of militant stories that were done in the sixties and the seventies. For the most part, the mass media is a class apart from America. They're richer than most. They certainly have more education than most. They have more influence and power than most. So they don't relate well to those that are outside of that circle of power.

Just look at the way the media covered recent prison "disturbances" very recently. There was... not a disturbance, but a rebellion, in Camp Hill, Pennsylvania, about 120 miles away from Huntingdon. Every official report pointed to overcrowding, and it really didn't deal with any other kinds of problems. The point is that when you look at the prisoners in Pennsylvania, at the prisoners anywhere, you're looking at a burgeoning population, busting out of the walls, just growing, growing, growing. People are being put two to a cell and doing life sentences, you know what I mean? What you have is a state and public attempt at a solution to a problem that is social, that is political. Very recently the Census Bureau said 31 million people were in poverty. Other records say that 3.1 million people are homeless in America. You've got people who do not have their basic needs fulfilled. They can't eat, they can't have shelter, they can't have clothing. And you have an infusion of drugs from Central America, which provides an economic incentive. So you have a lot of these people coming into these prisons from the inner city, who are African-American, who are Hispanic, Puerto Rican, Mexican-American out on the West Coast. But they find that it's an empty hole. There's nothing corrective being done to people in these jails. You can't correct people by putting them in a box, by denying them every right that the so-called Constitution gives to all so-called Americans. What you had at Camp Hill was a rebellion of the spirit. You had rebellion here, you had rebellion in Holmesburg prison in Philadelphia, you had fights in Graterford prison. All over this state. For several days you had men at Camp Hill Prison hand-cuffed and shackled together so that they couldn't wash, they couldn't relieve themselves, they couldn't eat. They couldn't do anything, and they were beaten by guards. If that's correction, what's repression?

Q: What about your own conditions here, and what has been your daily life?

MAJ: My daily life is 22 to 24 hours in the cell, in the cage, much like this joint here, except that it's got a toilet. No prison is a good prison. Some are better than others in small degrees. It's really internal to the prison. But all prisons are hell. I can't hold my children, hug my wife. So, I kind of tend to not address those kinds of things. It is personal. That is not to say that it ain't real. It's very real. The Bureau of Corrections instituted this policy in late 1982, I believe. There was no incident that precipitated it, by death row inmates. At that time, the Attorney General you're speaking of was the

Governor of Pennsylvania, and it was by his executive order, or order to the bureaucracy, that this little cage was constructed. No death row inmates have got involved with an escape attempt, or assault, or anything like that. There was a hostage taking in Graterford Prison in November 1981, but they were life prisoners, they were not death row prisoners. He used that, I'm told, as the justification to build the cage. That was one of the reasons why at least eight of us and other supporters had a hunger strike, in October of 1989, to try to draw attention to the conditions on death row.

I and other MOVE members in the Pennsylvania state have been in what's called "disciplinary custody": locked down in the holes, because we refuse to cut our hair and violate our faith, which is the teachings of John Africa. It's ironic that the state that was the birthplace of the Constitution and the Bill of Rights can deny the right of religion and faith to anyone, willy-nilly. In the State of Pennsylvania, there's what's called a MOVE stipulation that affects—not me, because of my sentence—but other MOVE prisoners who are eligible for parole. There are several prisoners who could be free today. They could go home if they agreed to stay away from MOVE people. The stipulation forbids Ramona Africa, for example, from going to any MOVE house in Philadelphia, from going to any courtroom in Philadelphia in which a MOVE trial is being conducted, from speaking to any reporter in any medium in Philadelphia on behalf of the MOVE organization. There's a stipulation imilar, but in a certain way more draconian, that they've used against a MOVE supporter named Richard Garland, who is at State Correction Institution in Pittsburgh. They said he can never visit Philadelphia. He cannot speak to any MOVE people. To understand MOVE is to understand that MOVE members are related to MOVE members, not just as brothers and sisters, of the same faith and the same organization, but as wives, husbands, children. Pennsylvania's government has created a condition of freedom in which a wife like Ramona Africa can't visit her MOVE husband if she wants to be free; can't visit her MOVE brothers; can't be family. And that's the cost of freedom. MOVE people have, to a man and woman, completely refused to abide by those conditions, with good reason. When a brother supporter, Richard Gaunt, up in Pittsburgh, was told that his condition of release and parole was that he never visit Philadelphia, he said, "Fine." He found a place to live in Pittsburgh, and a job, all of the conditions of the parole stipulation. Then he filed it with the parole board and they said, no, MOVE is a terrorist organization. They denied his parole, even in Pittsburgh. It seems to me that for the government of Pennsylvania, which funded, which conducted, which whitewashed and covered the May 13th bombing of MOVE to call MOVE people terrorist is like the pot calling the kettle black.

Q: Have they elaborated on that at all, calling MOVE a terrorist organization?

MAJ: Not at all, because other than the class-struggle defense notes, published by the Partisan Defense Committee, nothing has been published on that in America. So they can comfortably rely on the media to cover their tracks. The conditions that are put on MOVE people like Ramona Africa, Richard Garland, Sue Africa, Mo Africa and Carlos Africa, that spit in the face of the Pennsylvania and the United States Constitution. Those stipulations deny for MOVE people the right of assembly, the right of family, the right of association, the right of religion, every substantive right that you can think of—anyone is touched by those stipulations. So that in order for a MOVE person to be free, they have to surrender their rights to the state.

Q: What does that mean that you've been in disciplinary custody?

MAJ: It means that, for one thing, your reading material, or your books, are severely restricted. I can only get legal books, and very few religious books. It means that a book like the *Columbia History of the World* would be denied; Amnesty International's 1988 book on the death penalty will be and has been denied, because they don't want me to see it; it means I can't buy food, which may seem very trivial, but in prison all you can do is eat, you know.

Q: I imagine that being denied books is very hard for a journalist, too.

MAJ: It's quite hard for journalists. You try to read as many papers as you can, but radical papers, revolutionary papers, progressive papers, like *Revolutionary Worker* and *Burning Spear* are also censored. Not from a disciplinary position, but they don't want revolutionary material circulating in prisons and giving people insight into resistance in the empire.

Q: Why do you think there is a disproportionate number of African-Americans on death row?

MAJ: Well, it's really a national phenomenon. I read recently that one of the reasons why the Governor of Virginia, Doug Wilder, found it easy to accept the death penalty was that there was no longer a racial imbalance among people convicted and sentenced to death. When I read that, the words of the politician trying to seek this political office in Virginia, it didn't really ring true to me, so I ordered some books, legal books from the Bureau of Justice in Washington and looked up the statistics to find out just what they were. Virginia has a higher percentage of African-Americans on death row, compared to the population of African-Americans in the state; higher than the United States, and higher than many states in the United States. It approaches eighty percent. Here in Pennsylvania, Blacks are about nine percent of the population and we approach fifty-three percent on death row. Nationally, the population of Blacks in prison period is thirty-seven percent when we're thirteen percent of this nation's population. Clearly, just looking at the numbers, looking at the amount of Blacks in prison, on death row, we must address the racist nature of the criminal justice system. *The National Law Journal* and *Lexis* had a crime poll in August of 1989. It showed that eighty percent of Americans—whites and Blacks—agree that there's racism in the criminal justice system. Another figure that I read recently in the ABA Crisis in the Criminal Justice System Report is that there were over 34 million crimes, felonies, victimizations in America in 1986. Off hand, I'd like you to just give me a guess about how many went into the criminal justice system?

Q: I can't even guess.

MAJ: Thirty-one million out of 34 million were never exposed to arrest, never went into the criminal justice system at all. Unsolved, unreported. I had to read that a few times to try to understand what it was saying. It shows that the arrests, the convictions, the sentences, of hundreds of thousands of people in America are for purely symbolic value. When you really look at the numbers of crimes that are happening in America, prison doesn't even begin to touch the tip of the iceberg. When you talk about symbols, the death penalty comes readily to mind. Historically, and according to statistics published by the same government, the death penalty was found to be of the greatest utility for controlling Blacks. From the 1930's to 1980, specifically in the southern states, hundreds of people were put to death for rape. Ninty-eight percent of those people were Black people. You have never had a white man sentenced to death in America for raping a Black woman. You see what I'm saying? All of those things draw a very clear picture that the criminal justice system is itself a symbol, to give people a palliative—"We're doing something, we're taking care of something"—when it's really a farce, it's a fraud. I said earlier that there is no correction being done, in fact what's being done is corruption. You're destroying people's minds, you're creating monsters for tomorrow. You take a man, put him in a cage, deny him any right, any ability to grow; there's no teaching, there's no educational programs, there's no social programs, the only program is "lock 'em up." You either do one of two things in life: you grow or you retrogress. You don't stand still. Nothing in life stands still. So when these people in these jails go home, they'll be a problem again. You've created a problem that you cannot solve. That's one of the underlying reasons for the trouble at Camp Hill. You can talk about overcrowding all you want, but if you've got one man in one cage who's being treated like a dog and he can't stretch enough to grow, then you've got one man too much.

Q: How many people are on death row here?

MAJ: There are approximately 57 here at Huntingdon, and 115 state-wide. You have three death rows in the state of Pennsylvania, one at Graterford, about 15 miles outside of Philadelphia and one in the city of Pittsburgh. Huntingdon is the largest.

Q: So you're in solitary.

MAJ: Yes, we're locked in 24-hours-a-day. There is a yard, but since the "disturbances" here—the riot—people go out to the yard every other day if they wish. The yard is really cages. Ever see dog-pens? That's what they are. They're dog-pens with razor-wire around the top. Cyclone fences, little boxes. Cages. You can go out there and get fresh air for about two hours. This jail is like the Marion of Pennsylvania. Trouble-makers, radicals, they're sent here. And anybody who gets into a disturbance with a guard, they threaten: "Well, we're gonna send you to Huntingdon." "Oh no, not that!" That's what they do.

Q: What were these so-called disturbances?

MAJ: Well, it began with a man named Tim Forest who was brought over to the hole, which is a restricted housing unit, and beaten. Tim was well-liked by a lot of people in the jail and I think it infuriated them. Shortly thereafter there was a confrontation on the jail center—the jail is like a wheel with the center and spokes going off of it, the spokes being the block, the center being the control division. About 75 men converged on the center and told them: "Look, you gotta stop beatin' them guys up over there handcuffed and all that." Well, that was said, but it wasn't done. A few nights later, men were returning from eating out in population, and another confrontation occurred, this one more violent. At least thirty people were hospitalized. Broken bones, skull fractures. What is most remarkable is that the men were subdued and handcuffed to radiators, and then beaten, had their bones broken. Because no one could contact anyone. It really got buried out in this area. The only thing that was ever published about it was that there are disturbances at Huntingdon. Well, it was a small riot, but it got very vicious. Men were handcuffed and shackled, dragged from A-block to B-block, which is the restricted housing where death row is. Some were in their underwear, all were wet from the water-hoses, they were taken out into the cage I just told you about, in sub-zero temperatures, and left there for several hours. Several men suffered from exposure. The reality is that outside of letters to family or letters to politicians, that's a story that hasn't been told, it hasn't been reported. This region, because it is so outside of the big Philadelphia and Pittsburgh area, just snuffed it out, it never made wire services or anything. Also, because of Camp Hill, it was kind of overblown by the heat and fire and rage of Camp Hill in October of 1984.

I'd like to mention that there were three MOVE people at Camp Hill: Phil Africa, Eddie Africa and Chuckie Africa. Chuckie was in the hole, he had just been transferred two months before from Dallas Pennsylvania prison where he had just spent 65 months in the hole. He was in an isolated section, so he was not involved in the rebellions. But when troopers stormed the prison, they went to the isolated section and guards from Dallas prison attacked him, at least eight of them, and tried to break him up. He was chained, handcuffed, taken away from Camp Hill to Lewisburg prison, then to Atlanta prison, and now he's at Lapank in California. And it was not in our interest to be involved in that rebellion. It was not MOVE related. The point is, he was attacked because he was

145

a MOVE member, because he was Chuckie Africa, of the MOVE organization, and taken all the way across the country in a matter of days and isolated from his family, from his relatives, and supporters. Phil and Eddie Africa, my last report is that they're at Leavenworth in Kansas. I don't know anything about their conditions.... Talkin' to me?

Q: ...It might be that our time is nearly up, but I didn't hear them, and there's no one at the window.... What is the percentage of Black inmates here?

MAJ: Fifty-seven percent. And that's a very conservative percentage and I'll say why: that number comes from the Bureau of Corrections itself. According to the Bureau, if you're Hispanic, you're white. That might be a surprise to a few of these Puerto Rican brothers here who are probably as black as me in flesh, but according to the records, if someone has a Hispanic surname he's put in the white column. So I would say it's well over sixty percent. In terms of staff, I doubt if it's well over sixty percent Black, Afro-American and Hispanic. The point is that the prisoner is merely a commodity. What you have in America, in rural America, is the growth of prison industries. You've got parts of this country, like Huntindon, Pennsylvania, like this valley, this region, that exist on the monies that come from this prison. Most of rural America would die for an industry like corrections. They don't mean to correct people, to help people, to take someone and make them a better person somewhere down the line. That's not even part of the equation. They mean, secure a business that brings in three million dollars a year in sales. Corrections is as much an industry as McDonald's hamburgers. Instead of hamburgers you have people, you see what I'm saying. I just read in the paper about a rural New York State county actually lobbying the governor for a prison. There was a time when people would say, "Not in my backyard, we don't want a prison here." That time has gone. The big steel mills are gone, the big auto industries are gone, the big industries, the rust belt industries in America are gone overseas. So the newest industry is "corrections." The problem is, ain't nobody being corrected. Essentially, because it was born in corruption and continues to be corrupt, this system cannot correct. You've got three million people in the streets who can't find a place to live. It seems to me if you want to correct something, correct that situation. Find houses for people. You've got maybe 50 million people in America living in poverty today. You want to correct something, correct that situation. You'd have a better shot than with what you're doing here. When you have sickness, illness, theft, brutality by public officials, that's a radical situation. To bring it back into whack, into a natural bounds, is not radical, it's normal. It's like saying that if someone ate fresh fruit, that was a radical diet. In the real world, hamburger is a radical diet because of what you have to go through to get it. And so it's taking the reform out the situation and just going with what's natural, what God intended.

Q: Do you think that's a possibility?

MAJ: I think it's a necessity. It's not in terms of a possibility. People have to look at what's working and what ain't. It really ain't working for most of the people of the world. I talked a minute ago about 30 to 50 million people in poverty in America, but when you look at much of the middle class, they're one paycheck away from homelessness, one paycheck away from poverty. I've been there, I know how that feels. And the point is that this kind of life of quiet desperation from check to check is survival, it ain't life. It leaves no room for the person to look higher, to look deeper, to grow. When I was talking about all the brutality that was happening at Camp Hill, the beatings, and handcuffed and shackled prisoners, I recognize that the people who did the beatings did it for a paycheck. It was like, "It's nothin' personal, nigger." But it's got people so bent out of shape that they'll go in there and break a guy's bones, not because they hate the guy and not because the guy did something to them, but because they're getting paid.

Q: There seems to be a repetition in a number of the cases from the late sixties, through the seventies, into the eighties of political prisoners where there have been accusations of killing police or federal agents...

MAJ: Yes, because the police represent agents of the system, the defenders of the system. John Africa explains that the system will say that there's nothing wrong with the system pointing guns at people, but there's everything wrong with people pointing guns at the system. Implicit within that is that no one can defend themselves. The system can liquidate people willy-nilly, with no one saying a word. And they can. They did it on May 13th, 1985. People were liquidated by the state on May 13th, 1985 but no one got convicted of murder, of mass murder, of providing instruments of crime. No one got convicted except Ramona Africa, for survival. Because survival is a crime.

Q: You had talked about "by any means necessary." I wanted to bring up the issues of self-defense and using arms because we shouldn't skirt around those issues.

MAJ: I believe that it's a natural right and principle of life for all people to defend themselves. I believed it when I got exposed to the MOVE organization, I believe it now. Self-defense is a natural right and no one can take that away from you. To suggest otherwise is to place your right to defend yourself in someone else's hands, in whose heart your best interests may not lie. If we believe what we said a few moments ago about the U.S. government bringing drugs to get funds for the contras, then those aren't the kind of people you want defending you, are they?

Q: How about the issue of people who have actually used armed struggle just in a sense of a symbolic bombing?

MAJ: Like the resistance conspiracy defendants?

Q: And the Ohio Seven.

MAJ: The Ohio Seven. They hurt property, and unfortunately in America property is God. They would have gotten less time if they were to bomb, say, an abortion clinic, or if they had really hurt people. I read about the Ohio Seven cases, and the resistance conspiracy cases, and the kind of time they've gotten. So when you look at abortion clinic bombings, it's incredible. It is a political response, because of their political position. The Ohio Seven are made examples because of their political orientation and political beliefs.

Q: Did you hear that the Ohio Seven were actually acquitted of seditious conspiracy?

MAJ: Yes I did. I was quite surprised. They did a lot of work among the people, and they worked very hard at the trial. They deserve it that way. They did well, very well.

Q: Even in symbolic bombings there's always a risk of innocent people getting hurt. I guess the Brinks incident becomes the most prominent example. Do you have any position on those sorts of issues?

MAJ: I believe that people should do whatever they feel driven to do to support their position. You know, MOVE's position is a little different, and I must distinguish that. Sue Africa, Mo Africa, Carlos Africa, are now serving time in prison for taking up arms to defend MOVE headquarters in West Philadelphia on May 20th, 1977, a case for which there was an incredible response by the city. I'm talking 700 cops, a siege around the neighborhood, and it really continued day by day, until it built into the August 8th, 1978 police assault on MOVE headquarters with maybe 500 policemen. What people may not know is that the arms that MOVE had were inoperable. They were there to show police that MOVE was serious about defending their own, but they had no firing vans, they couldn't work. As for bombing and stuff like that, MOVE has never been involved in that, so I would be real hesitant to take that position. MOVE people have been charged with that but they've never proven any of that....Who was that?

Q: The guard.

MAJ: The guard?

Q: She said ten minutes.

MAJ: She's right on time.

The Prison-House of Nations

Q: Why did you leave the BPP and when was that?

MAJ: I don't remember in terms of when. You know, I don't put a lot of stock in those years and dates and all—it would drag me down. The reasons were some personal, but some political. Around the time of the fight between the East Coast and the West Coast Panthers, I felt that it was not my function, when I joined the Party, or my reason behind joining it, to fight other Black Panthers. I felt that it was proper to fight the system, but when the system can manipulate you into fighting your own, then the system wins and the people lose. I think that the period really reflected the destruction of the Party as a national presence, because once it was split between coasts—between the Central Committee and reigning Party members of the West Coast and some of the most active chapters of the East Coast—then for all intents and purposes it lost its effectiveness, because even though the Party began in the West, some of its most energetic and militant chapters existed in the East, because this is where some of the largest Black communities exist, and where some of the most dire

---

Interview from death row in Huntingdon Prison, Pennsylvania, October 1992.

conditions exist and hence the need for a Black Panther Party was very strong here—like Philadelphia, like the Winston-Salem, Baltimore and New Haven chapters. Once that was split asunder, it could no longer function as the Black Panther Party, no matter what name it used. It was no longer a united Black political revolutionary organization trying to achieve Black political power—Black revolutionary political power I should add.

Q: How would you describe your situation after you left the BPP? Did you feel that journalism was a way to go about political aims?

MAJ: In some respects I did. It is true to the extent that journalism is a tool to change people's consciousness, a tool to give people insight, and in another way a kind of affirmation that their lives have value and purpose. When one reads the daily press or listens to what is broadcasted on the regular "white" radio stations and TV stations, you will perceive a picture, a slanted picture of Black life that reflects it in the most improper terms. When media journalism and propaganda is used to reflect a positive side of people, the side of people resisting oppression, the side of people's inherent worth, no matter what their property or economic value is, then that in itself is revolutionary, because this system tends to denigrate people who are poor—when most of the people on the planet earth are poor. And they have inherent worth as human beings, as beings on this planet. That is the kind of consciousness that drove me towards journalism. Other than the fact, of course, that through the Party I was trained in that field and was able to write from a radical revolutionary perspective.

Q: When did you first meet MOVE?

MAJ: Even prior to doing broadcast work, of course, I read about them in the newspaper like most people in Philadelphia and had seen one or two MOVE people on the street. But when the confrontation started heating up in Philadelphia in 1977 and 1978—and it was really a very naked level of repression that the Philadelphia police heaped on MOVE—I could not help but draw attention to that, as a reporter. The acting mayor of Philadelphia at the time, Frank Rizzo, and his police started a siege against a MOVE house in Powelton Village in 1977. The siege lasted over one year. By the end, police cut off all water and electricity to the house, but people from the neighborhood and supporters from the city supplied MOVE with the basic necessities. Finally, on August 8th, 1978 more than 700 policemen stormed the house. During their action one policeman was hit in the cross-fire of his colleagues. Nine MOVE members who were arrested in the house were later charged and convicted of having jointly killed this one cop. They were all sentenced to 30-100 years in prison, despite the fact that the judge admitted that he didn't know who had shot the cop.

Coming from the quasi-socialist background and in some respects paramilitary background of the Party, my first impressions of MOVE were extraordinarily negative. I could not perceive them as revolutionary, because they didn't wear the uniforms, of course like the Panthers did. They weren't talking about Marxism–Leninism–Mao Tse-Tung thought as the Panthers were doing. They weren't talking about building a socialist society as a solution to the economic, political and social problems that exist in the U.S.

So, again, in the same way that the Philadelphia Police Department beat me into the BPP, the Philadelphia Police Department's repression of MOVE attracted me to MOVE. Because even though the repression was extraordinarily severe, brutal and devastating, MOVE continued to rebel and resist, and as MOVE founder John Africa would say, "Strength and commitment is attractive."

Q: Can you say how it came about that you went on trial for allegedly having killed a cop? Do you feel that the Philadelphia police set you up on the night of the incident, December 9th, 1981, when you were shot and this cop got killed?

MAJ: I think it is undeniable that elements of a set-up existed and that my background as a Panther and as what some people called a "MOVE journalist" or a MOVE supporter were elements involved in that. There was never any time before or after when the police acted as if they didn't know who I was. For several months—the better part of a year, when I worked at a public radio station—I was actually stationed right next door to the Philadelphia Police Department's headquarters, so that every day, for several times a day, I had to go that route to go to work. That said, I think that the work that I did put me down as a target to be neutralized. One must look back at the coverage of MOVE around the police siege of the MOVE house in 1978 to see how demonized, how inhumane, how animalistic in the most negative sense MOVE was portrayed to be. When interviews were done with them that showed that they were good, decent and committed people, it challenged the public perception of who they were. I did these interviews because I thought they needed to be done; I did them because I thought it was the right thing to do; and I did them because I thought that any other journalist should have been doing them. If someone else would have done it, I would have had no need to do it.

I remember going to MOVE headquarters and making

some phone calls, and going back to the job and being criticized by my boss for that. When I asked him why, he said that phone taps on MOVE headquarters had revealed that I had made several calls from there. I said "So what? I can call from wherever I want to call." And he said: "Well, it damages your objectivity. Other reporters are calling you Mumia Africa." He meant that as a slur. So it is very clear that police intelligence, but not only that, also intrastation intelligence, had me marked as a MOVE operative, when it simply wasn't true. I was just a reporter who worked closely with his subjects.

Q: Do you believe that racism played a role in the fact that you were sentenced to death?

MAJ: What I believe is really immaterial. I think that the facts speak for themselves when one takes note of the fact that the state by intent and design selected a predominantly white jury, a predominantly older, middle-aged jury, jurors who for the most part hailed from what is called Northeast Philadelphia, which is a predominantly very, very white part of town. Some jurors were related to cops, some jurors were actually friends of cops. Also, when one takes into account the intentional removal of African-Americans from the central city from the jury, I don't think any other result can come to mind.

Q: Do you see racism in general being reflected in the death penalty? How does it play out?

MAJ: Let's look at it this way: of the about 2,800 people who are on death rows across the U.S., an estimated forty percent are African-Americans, for the most part men—of the 2,800 people only 28 are women. So forty percent are Black men. The percentage of African-Americans in society is roughly 12 percent, but when you slice it into half by male and female you are talking about six percent. So six percent of the population become an estimated forty percent on death row. I don't think that those results can be obtained by any way without racism being a factor. At all levels of the criminal justice system—at the charging level, the prosecution level, the judging level and the defense level, not to mention the whole level of appeal—mostly white individuals in positions of power like magistrates, district attorneys, judges and appellate judges and defense lawyers etcetera make independent determinations about the worth of a person, the worth of their life and whether they should be exposed to the most extreme penalty. More often than not, when an African-American is placed in that position, all bets are off.

Q: What is your impression of the rebellion in L.A.? Do you think that this is just one spark, which was quieted down, or do you feel that there is a potential that the African-American community will start organizing around police brutality again?

MAJ: I really believe in some respects some level of organizing has already begun as a response to L.A. But the L.A. rebellions reflect more than anything else hopelessness. When people riot, they riot because they feel they have nothing to lose. Riot is an act of desperation, not of intent, not of planning. I just think that the forces that converge on African-American life from all levels of American society were symbolized in that case where Rodney King was beaten and his tormentors were acquitted by—people say a predominantly white jury—that was an *all*-white jury. I think people in L.A. responded viscerally, in their guts to what they knew was an injustice and it was a slap in the face of African-American people. Did it move people to organize? I think in some respects, yes. It showed that this system is not our system. It showed that when one is an employee or an agent of the system like a cop, that the system will bend over backwards to protect those who are charged with assaulting someone or even killing someone, if that person is poor, African-American, without power, without influence or the like. I think it shows also how arrogant the system is. I mean one would think they would bend over backwards the other way when there is a videotape of the crime, but it meant absolutely nothing, as if it had happened in the dark of night, as if there was no videotape capturing this. But there it was and it meant absolutely nothing. A lot of people, well maybe not a lot but some people tend to take heart from the fact that the federal government stepped in after the rebellions to say, now we are going to start a federal prosecution. When you really look at it, this is the same federal government that years before had promised that they would make an investigation of that kind of behavior across the nation. And for years there was silence.

Q: Often now the heads of police departments or the mayors of large cities like New York and L.A. are African-Americans who have been in power a number of years now. Do you think that the majority of the African-American community has a perception that here are members of their own community in positions of power and they obviously don't change the methods very much?

MAJ: I think that most folks in the African-American community know in their hearts and in their minds that there is a difference between the appearance of power and true power, that African-American political leaders can be mayors, police commissioners, governors, prison superintendants, they can have a position of power and lack real power. Power is the ability to enforce your will. When one looks at what happened in Philadelphia in 1985 under Mayor Goode and in New York in September of this year under Mayor Dinkins respectively, one cannot come away from these situations without feeling that in some respects they were absolutely powerless. In the Goode situation I refer to the May 13th, 1985 bombing of MOVE, when police bombed and burned 11 MOVE people to death and burned a whole neighborhood. Mayor Goode accepted all the responsibility, but none of the blame. What he said lately in his recently published autobiography, *In Good Faith,* was that the reason why he was not on the scene in Osage Avenue when police bombed and then incinerated and shot down MOVE people was that he had received intelligence that the Philadelphia Police Department had marked him for death. I believe him, especially when you look at an event that happened very recently, when 10,000 policemen rioted in New York City and hurled racial slurs at their commander-in-chief, at the mayor of the city. Well, I don't care what your title is, if 10,000 people can come up to your office and call you a bathroom attendant, call you everything but a child of God, then you have no power. It shows the powerlessness of those people who are invested with power, because they cannot enforce their will. For instance, it is unthinkable that any white mayor or chief executive in a political system could be threatened with death by people who are his subordinates and that that white political figure would not have the skills or the contacts or the executive powers to isolate that threat and take care of it. None of these skills were demonstrated by Goode or Dinkins, who are for all intents and purposes fairly good politicians. But they happen to be

African-American politicians, who have the appearance of power, but no real power.

Q: But twenty years ago, African-Americans struggled to be represented in the political arena and demanded control over their communities, and on the surface this demand seems to have been met.

MAJ: Well, twenty years ago one of the goals of the Black Panther Party was the achievement of Black revolutionary political power. The Party made a distinction between Black revolutionary political power and Black political power, so that simply putting a Black face in a high place was not a solution. In a very real sense, when an African-American person is placed in a position of power, he or she doesn't represent the interests of the poor, of the powerless; he or she represents the interests of the system and not the people. So if you look back twenty years ago the prospect of a Black mayor of New York or a Black mayor of Philadelphia for that matter, or even of a Black police commissioner was almost unthinkable. Now it is thinkable, but the reality is that for people in the real world on the streets life has not changed for the better—in fact, in some respects it has probably changed for the worse.

Q: Can you describe what your legal situation is right now?

MAJ: We are preparing for a post-conviction relief petition. I am working with my attorneys on that. One of my attorneys, at least, Leonard Weinglass from New York, has said, very accurately in my estimation, that for intents and purposes I have never had any true representation. When you have a lawyer who is appointed, who doesn't want to be there or is denied just the most fundamental tools of defense, then you have a lawyer in name, but in name only. *The Philadelphia Enquirer,* Philadelphia's biggest mainstream newspaper, recently did a report that dealt with the representation of people who are charged with capital offenses in Philadelphia. What was revealed was that Philadelphia was at the bottom of the realm: that in, let's say Cleveland, Ohio or San Francisco, as a matter of course one would be supplied with two attorneys—one for the penalty phase and one for the guilt phase—along with jury selection specialists, a staff psychiatrist, a ballistician and an investigator. This is a matter of course, it goes with the program. Lawyers from those cities who are defending capital cases get $10,000 at the very bottom to begin; lawyers from Philadelphia, at least in the early '80s, got $2,500 tops. Now, I hear it has improved somewhat. The lawyer of someone who is charged with a capital offense in Philadelphia might get $4,500, but that is the highest that's ever been. They are also appointed by the judge, so that just as a matter of simple pop psychology or even politics—if I am the judge and I am going to appoint you to the case, and I also determine how much you get paid, when you get paid or even if you get paid, then you better not do anything that will make me look questionable or bad.

Q: As I understand it, right now you are being held in disciplinary custody because you refuse to cut your hair, which would be against your religious principles. Now the Commissioner of Corrections of Pennsylvania, Joseph Lehmann, has issued two new directives in regard to prison conditions for death-row prisoners and prisoners in disciplinary custody. Could you describe how your already extremely

160

harsh prison conditions are going to be restricted even further by those new directives?

MAJ: In a nutshell, the worst conditions on death row in America are just about to get worse. There are two new directives that are coming out of Harrisburg, Pennsylvania's capitol: Directives 801 and 802, which further restrict visitation, correspondence, letters, magazines and newspapers. To those who write directives in Harrisburg, apparently if one is locked up 22 hours a day, that is one hour too many out of your cell, so they are cutting it down to 23 hours a day locked up and one hour outside of the cell in a steel cage. For those in disciplinary custody, like myself, it will be one non-contact visit a month, no phone calls at all, one newspaper—a legal newspaper only, and one must give an old newspaper to get the next one. The only commissary available is two packs of cigarettes a month.

Q: What about stamps and papers, can you get that?

MAJ: No. No stamps, no papers, no envelopes... When I said only, I meant only. According to the directive, the only stuff that a person can purchase in this new status is one pack of cigarettes every two weeks or two packs of cigarettes a month. That's it. No soap, no shampoo, no nothing.

Q: There have been prison rebellions in Pennsylvania throughout the last two years. Do you think this is going to spark new resistance?

MAJ: It is difficult to predict in prison, because of course these new directives only apply in what is called restrictive housing units. Since those people in restrictive housing units are already the most restricted in prison, it is very rare for any overt resistance to occur in those kinds of units. For instance, when the riots did happen in Pennsylvania, they happened in population. In fact they happened in one of the most medium security prisons in Pennsylvania called Camp Hill. So, it's always difficult to predict how people are going to react. One of the things the Department of Corrections has done is to kind of give people several months' prior warning of the change by passing out to all inmates memos from the Department of Corrections about Directives 801 and 802, and a week ago passing out the actual text 801 and 802, so that people know what it is going to be. So, instead of being kind of a shock thing, it will be more of a phase situation. My guess is that's to ease it in on people, as opposed to a shock— one day this, the next day another. So, I don't know what is going to happen.

It brings certain things to mind from African-American history, especially the case of El-Hajj Malik El-Shabbaz, known popularly as Malcolm X, that when he was imprisoned his behavior was so negative that people called him by the name "Satan." It was only through his ability to study the teachings of the Honorable Elijah Muhammad and his ability to study a dictionary that he was able to pull himself out of that dark well of negativity and begin to build a positive core of self-being. That he did so is a tribute to his teachings as well as to his internal spirit, himself, his determination to come out of that well and to become something other than what society told him he was. Under these new directives he would not be able to receive those teachings. He would not be able to have a dictionary. So that one who was called "Satan" would never have been able to develop and metamorphose into a Malcolm X and later on El-Hajj Malik El-Shabbaz, because he would not be able to have the tools to develop, to

162

grow, to read, to stretch, to learn. If one looks at how the state is developing its new "Marionization" program [Marion is the maximum-maximum-security federal prison for men in Illinois, internationally infamous for its isolation program—eds.], it looks as if one of its intents is to stop that kind of growth and development and indeed to create, if not "Satans," then certainly beasts, bitter, angry, just burnt-up people as opposed to people who are growing, sensitive, insightful, better people. It seems to me that a system that dares call itself the Department of Corrections has a job to make people better as opposed to bitter.

Q: Your lawyers recently met with the Chief Counsel for Pennsylvania's Governor Robert Casey. Casey himself seems to claim that he still doesn't know anything about your case, despite the massive international and nationwide campaign on your behalf. What is your assessment of that meeting?

MAJ: Having heard that the Governor knew nothing about my case was shocking. The fact that Governor Casey could have no knowledge about the questions in regard to my case and my situation that were raised to him in New York at Cooper Union on October 2nd, 1992—despite the fact that thousands of people around the world signed petitions or wrote letters—whether they were distinquished members of Congress, members of the European Parliament or heads of international organizations and everyday people, common people who simply wrote and signed petitions—was shocking at best. It reflects, I think, the executive and political distance that politicians assume when they can be so separated from people that they actually hear nothing or perhaps only what they want to hear or hear perhaps only what their handlers and their people want them to hear. But it was shocking.

Q: What do you feel people both in the U.S. and in Europe should do to support you and other death row prisoners?

MAJ: That's a good question, but it must be looked at now in light of what has gone on in the past, how effective it has been or how inneffective it has been and perhaps new strategies have to be developed to ensure that never again can someone say "Well, I've only had 50,000 letters. I don't know anything." I don't know—that needs to be thought through, struggled on, analyzed and then strategized.

Q: A lot of people seem to think once Clinton gets into office everything will be better. From your perspective, is that true?

MAJ: Well, my perspective is a little biased. As an African-American on death row I am not of that opinion. I would suspect that for most Blacks and perhaps some white people on death row in Arkansas, I don't think they feel very heartened by that prospect, since Clinton is a staunch supporter of the death penalty and has been responsible for at least four executions in Arkansas. Clinton also calls for police and the building of new jails, despite the fact that there are already one million people in prisons throughout the U.S., which makes it the country with the highest incarceration rate worldwide in regard to its overall population.

Speaking of a larger community, I think that changes in a very real, everyday way will be minimal. One of the things that I read recently—for now, I'm still able to get newspapers, fortunately—was that both Governor Clinton and the incumbent President Bush were in favor of the new North American Free Trade Act (NAFTA) that has been passed between

Mexico, Canada and the U.S. One of the reasons why there is such high unemployment and joblessness in the U.S., that will surely be exasperated by the NAFTA pact, is that industry is fleeing the U.S. for a larger profit margin abroad. When one considers for instance that a pair of Reeboks sells for $75 and costs only $5.25 to produce in Indonesia, well then as a shoe manufacturer you're going to go where the labor is cheapest and where the raw materials that you need to gather are cheaper, where you don't have unions, where you don't have people saying we need a decent wage to live on. And that is overseas. If the pact happens you are going to see a flood of American businesses go right across the border to Mexico and snuggle up close to the border so that they can import into the U.S. Most of the businesses that have been here for generations are going to go where the profit margin is better. Working people who have built their lives on factory jobs, manufacturing and industrial type labor are going to have a problem. So, it will change the ways and welfare of everyday people for the worse.

Q: Do you at this point see any force out there that has a revolutionary strategy or the power to move people into action? And if not, what would it require to have that?

MAJ: There several organizations in the U.S. of varying ideological persuasions who have revolutionary theories that they believe will transform America's present social, political and economic reality. Do they have the power to enforce them and change the reality now? No. What it's going to take, more than anything, is the cohesion of many forces, the building of mass power to change those realities, in the sense that no one organization has the power to transform it themselves. This is a vast country with 260 million people and to suppose that an organization of 200, 300 people is going to affect the deep degrees of transformation that need to take place, is pretentious. Look at the fact that at its height the BPP had 15,000, 16,000 members and was cooperating with other revolutionary organizations as well.

When I talked about NAFTA and the free-trade agreement, what I was really referring to is that no matter whether the Democrats or the Republicans are in power, big business is going to run them like a puppet-master. They are now dancing to the tune not of the people, not of the millions of people who are out of work, but to big business interests. There are an estimated 3 million people in the U.S. who literally do not have a home to live in; they are not listening to those wails and cries and lamantations; what they are listening to is the heartbeat of Wall Street, because that is what runs political campaigns in America today. Unless and until a political gathering and grouping is able to galvanize the power of the masses of the people, then no immediate change is imminent—that is, positive change. There is going to be a whole lot of negative change to come. One of those changes is what we talked about earlier: Marionization. We are not just talking about the Marionization of this prison here in Huntingdon or in Pennsylvania prisons, but the Marionization and the "prisonization" of America. You have over one million people locked up in prisons and jails in the U.S. right now. Indeed if we were to break that down into percentages, over 38% of that million are African-American men who come from six percent of the U.S. population. So unless and until popular force is built and wielded that coheres something from here and something there, a popular force that develops a counterforce to the "mainstream" for real, then there will be no change. What you are looking at in the U.S. when I say prisonization is not just the million people who are locked down, but increasingly, as industries flee this country, people find that their only option in terms of personal survival is to become a part of what has been called a "fortress economy." Increasingly, when people look for jobs, they are finding jobs in the security field, that is as prison guards, as cops, etc. So from both the outside and the inside America is becoming the prison-house of nations.

Q: Why do think it was that for many years people even on the left or in the African-American community have not heard about political prisoners, and in particular about Black Panther and BLA political prisoners like you or Bashir Hameed or Nuh Washington from the BLA?

MAJ: I guess the reason is simple. In American consciousness, as well as in African-American consciousness, something is not real unless it's on TV. If it didn't happen on NBC, CBS or CNN, it didn't happen. Marshall McLuhan said "The medium is the message," and it is. That which the ruling class's communications network wishes to present and promote, that is what is carried over into popular consciousness; that which it does not wish to promote, it either ignores or slanders. When you talk about the African-American community, of course, if someone were to estimate the amount of hours that people watch TV across racial lines, African-American youth and women watch more TV than anybody in the U.S. I just read from the *Harpers* "Index" a few days ago that the ten shows most viewed by Blacks are not even in the top ten of those viewed by whites. So that they are actually looking at different kinds of shows, but they are still looking at shows which come from a perspective that sells soap, that sells products, that sells this system and its way of life in every frame, in every stanza. People like myself, like Bashir

Hameed, like Abdul Majid, like Geronimo ji-Jaga Pratt, like Chuckie Africa and Delbert Africa from MOVE, like all these political prisoners, are invisible to millions of Americans.

Court Transcript

Present: Joseph McGill, Assistant District Attorney for the Commonwealth and Anthony Jackson, Counsel for the Defense (Court-Appointed).

MR. JACKSON: Your Honor, with your approval the defense would call Mumia Abu-Jamal.

THE COURT: Do you want to take the stand? (Whereupon the defendant approaches the Bar of the Court.)

BY THE COURT CRIER: (To Defendant at the Bar of the Court:)

Q. Would you state your full name for the record, please?

A. Mumia Abu-Jamal.

(At 10:34 a.m. the Defendant was affirmed of record.)

DEFENDANT JAMAL: I would like to read a statement.

Testimony given before Judge Albert F. Sabo on July 3, 1982 in the Court of Common Pleas, Criminal Division, City Hall, Philadelphia.

THE COURT: Mr. Jackson, do you want to question him?

MR. JACKSON: Mr. Jamal would you have something to say to the Court?

DEFENDANT JAMAL: I would.

THE COURT: Fine.

DEFENDANT JAMAL: Today's decision comes as no surprise. In fact, many will remember that I said this would happen last week when John Africa predicted and prophesied this jury's decision. I want everyone to know it came after a legal, trained lawyer was imposed upon me against my will. A legal, trained lawyer whose interests were clearly not my own. A legal, trained lawyer named Tony Jackson, a man who knew he was inadequate to the task, and chose to follow the direction of this black-robed conspirator, Albert Sabo, even if it meant ignoring my directions.

To quote John Africa, "When a lawyer chooses to follow the conditions of the court, he compromises his obligations to his 'client'."

It was a legal, trained lawyer who followed Sabo's direction not to introduce the testimony of Policeman Gary Wakshul, a cop who, according to his statement of 12-9-82, arrested me, carried me to a wagon, accompanied me to Jefferson Hospital, guarded me, and returned to Homicide later that morning to make a statement. According to Wakshul, quote: "We stayed with the male at Jefferson until we were relieved. During this time, the negro male made no comments." According to Wakshul's statement of February the 11th, 1982, over 2 months later, Wakshul recalls, "Oh, yeah, Jamal said: 'I shot him, I hope the M.F. dies'." Did he not consider that a "comment"? According to Sabo, Wakshul is on vacation, so despite the fact his testimony is directly linked to a supposed confession, he would not be called in to testify. How convenient. It was a legal, trained lawyer who told the jury, "You have heard all the evidence," knowing that wasn't so. The jury heard merely what Sabo allowed — nothing more. Many jurors were told I would cross-examine witnesses, make opening and closing arguments, and explore evidence. What they also heard was that I would act as my own attorney, my own lawyer. What they saw was a man silenced, gagged by judicial decree. So what they heard was nothing.

A man ordered not to fight for his life. Every so-called "right" was deceitfully stolen from me by Sabo. My demand that the defense assistance of my choice, John Africa, be allowed to sit at the defense table was repeatedly denied. While, meanwhile, in a City Hall courtroom just four floors directly above, a man charged with murder sits with his lawyer, and his father, who just happens to be a Philadelphia policeman. The man, white, was charged with beating a black man to death, and came to court to have his bail revoked, after being free for several weeks. His bail was revoked after a public outcry in the black community about the granting of a bail at all. Of course, my bail, a ransom of $250,000, was revoked one day after it was issued. For one defendant everything is granted. For another, everything is denied.

But, isn't justice blind, equal in its application?...

Does it matter whether a white man is charged with killing a black man or a black man is charged with killing a white man? As for justice, when the prosecutor represents the Commonwealth, the judge represents the Commonwealth and the court-appointed lawyer is paid and supported by the

Commonwealth, who follows the wishes of the defendant, the man charged with the crime? If the court-appointed lawyer ignores or goes against the wishes of the man he's charged with representing, whose wishes does he follow?

Who does he truly represent or work for? To again quote John Africa: "When you judges hang a person, put a person in an electric chair, gas a person, shoot a person to death for a crime you all didn't see that person commit, you ain't solving the problem of the crime, of the so-called criminal or the victim. You've caused a burden for the mother that is now without a son, the wife that is now without a husband, the daughter that is now without a father and society for putting faith in this goddamning procedure, for it is the system that is guilty of the crimes; of all that is criminal. All crimes are committed within the system, not without, because the influence of that ignorant black boy you judges gassed to death, poor white boy you judges shot to death, unaware Puerto Rican boy, girl, adult you judges electrocuted to death came straight from you judges, your bosses, their crimes. In short, this system." A quotation from John Africa.

I am innocent of these charges that I have been charged with and convicted of, and despite the connivance of Sabo, McGill and Jackson to deny me my so-called rights to represent myself, to assistance of my choice, to personally select a jury who's totally of my peers, to cross-examine witnesses, and to make both opening and closing arguments, I am still innocent of these charges.

According to your so-called law, I do not have to prove my innocence. But, in fact, I did have to by disproving the Commonwealth's case. I am innocent despite what you 12 people think and the truth shall set me free.

This jury is not composed of my peers, for those closest to my life experiences were intentionally and systematically

172

excluded, peremptorily excused. Only those prosecution prone, some who began with a fixed opinion of guilt, some related to City Police, mostly white, mostly male remain. May they one day be so fairly judged.

Long live John Africa!! for his assistance in this fight for my life. It is John Africa who has strenghtened me, aided me, and guided me, and loved me! Could John Africa have done worse than this worthless sellout and shyster who promised much and delivered nothing? Could he have done worse than Tony Jackson?

It was John Africa's influence that this Court feared and his assistance that this Court resisted, and denied, as if it were unfair to have him help me fight for my life. It is his protection that remains despite this Court's resistance and opinion.

On December the 9th, 1981, the police attempted to execute me in the street. This trial is a result of their failure to do so. Just as police tried to kill my brothers and sisters of the Family Africa on August the 8th, 1978, they failed, and hence, a so-called trial was conducted to complete the execution. But, Long Live John Africa for our continued survival!

This decision today proves neither my guilt nor my innocence. It proves merely that the system is finished. Babylon is falling!! Long Live MOVE!! Long Live John Africa!

(There was a conference between
Counsel for the Defense and the Defendant.)

MR. JACKSON: I have no further questions, Your Honor.

MR. McGILL: May I proceed, Your Honor?

THE COURT: Go ahead.

MR. McGILL: Perhaps it would be better, Your Honor, if I would stand over here and direct my comments to him.

THE COURT: I don't care.

MR. McGILL: It seems kind of silly if I turn to the right.

(Whereupon the District Attorney stands at the witness box, directing his cross-examination to the Defendant.)

MR. McGILL: I will not be that long, Ladies and Gentlemen.

MR. JACKSON: Your Honor, can we see you at side-bar for just one moment, please?

(The following colloquy occurred at side-bar.)

MR. JACKSON: Your Honor, I know, of course—I am anticipating—I believe Mr. McGill has a number of newspaper articles and publications and perhaps other quotations. I would object to the authority purportedly attributed or if attributed to the defendant, if they are not authenticated or without authentification and without any acknowledgement or truth, but, simply, to the defendant himself. I would object to the questioning in that even if he asked the question, "Did you say so-and-so," whatever his answer is, or is going to be, it's already prejudiced the minds and inflamed the jury and I would object to the reading of anything that is purported to be from the defendant.

MR. McGILL: This is a sentencing hearing, Judge.

THE COURT: Yes.

MR. McGILL: And any kind of a statement that is made by the defendant, the purpose of the authentification, I would authenticate it, is what the defendant would say, the actions that would result or —strike that—

Actually, what the defendant would say because of — or, that he would adopt it or not, I think that would be entirely up to the determining factors as to whether or not the evidence is admissible. I think he has opened up an extensive amount of doors. I can't begin to count them in the statement, including the inadmissible testimony or the inadmissible evidence, or documents and quoting of people, John Africa, among others. There are so many doors open, Judge, that really —

MR. JACKSON: Well, that is his prerogative to project or not to project, but — and to go into that, but an unauthenticated document —

THE COURT: You knew that Mr. Abu-Jamal had the statement prepared and you knew that he was going to read it regardless whether the District Attorney objected or not, so it seems in point that I will allow him to cross-examine him.

Go ahead.

(The above concluded the side-bar conference.)

(In Open Court)

MR. McGILL: Mr. Jackson, do you have a copy of that statement that he read?

MR. JACKSON: No, I don't.

MR. McGILL: Okay,

CROSS EXAMINATION BY MR. McGILL:

Q. Mr. Jamal, what was the first quote you made that John Africa had stated — I think that might have been on your first page?

A. Why don't you ask the stenographer?

Q. Do you have it in front of you, the document that you read?

A. I sure do.

Q. Would you take a look at it and tell me what that says?

A. I said, why don't you ask the stenographer.

Q. Well, is there any particular reason why you don't want to respond to my question, sir?

A. (No answer)

Q. Let me try something else, then.
What is the reason you did not stand when Judge Sabo came into the courtroom?

MR. JACKSON: Objection.

THE COURT: Overruled.

DEFENDANT ABU-JAMAL: Because Judge Sabo deserves no honor from me or anyone else in this courtroom because he operates — because of the force, not because of right. (Whereupon the defendant stands up at Defense Counsel's table.) Because he is an executioner. Because he is a hangman; that's why.

BY MR. McGILL:

Q. You are not an executioner?

A. No. (Whereupon the defendant sits at Defense Counsel's table.) Are you?

Q. Mr. Jamal, let me ask you if you can recall saying something some time ago and perhaps it might ring a bell as to whether or not you are an executioner or endorse such actions. "Black brothers and sisters—and organizations—which wouldn't commit themselves before are relating to us Black People that they are facing—we are facing the reality that the Black Panther Party has been facing, which is—" Now, listen to the quote. You've often been quoted saying this: "Political power grows out of the barrel of a gun." Do you remember saying that, sir?

A. I remember writing that. That's a quotation from Mao Tse-Tung.

Q. There is also a quote —

A. Let me respond if I may?

Q. Well, let me ask you a question.

A. Let me respond fully. I was not finished when you continued.

Q. All right, continue.

A. Thank you.

Q. Continue to respond, then, please, sir.

A. That was a quotation from Mao Tse-Tung of the Peoples' Republic of China. It's very clear that political power grows out of the barrel of a gun or else America wouldn't be here today. It is America who has seized political power from the Indian race, not by God, not by Christianity, not by goodness, but by the barrel of a gun.

Q. Do you recall making that quote, Mr. Jamal, to Acel Moore?

A. I recall quoting Mao Tse-Tung to Acel Moore about 12 to 15 years ago.

Q. Do you recall saying: "All power to the people"? Do you recall that?

A. "All power to the people"?

Q. Yes.

A. Yes. (Nods head affirmatively.)

178

Q. Do you believe that your actions as well as your philosophy are consistent with the quote: "Political power grows out of the barrel of a gun"?

A. I believe that America has proven that quote to be true.

Q. Do you recall saying that: "The Panther Party is an uncompromising party, it faces reality"?

A. (Nods head affirmatively.) Yes. Why don't you let me look at the article so I can look at it in its full context, as long as you're quoting?

Q. I'd be very glad to give you the article. I am ashamed—I'm kind of sorry you didn't—I'm kind of sorry you didn't give me your statement before.

A. Well, you can't have everything I have.

Q. Here is your statement, sir. Do you recall saying this when you had the name Wes Cook?

A. Well, let me look at it.
(Whereupon the District Attorney presents the newspaper article to the Defendant who examines same.)
I would like to read the entire article if you have no objection.

MR. McGILL: Go right ahead.

DEFENDANT JAMAL: Okay. Do you have the continuation, page 12, column 1?

MR. McGILL: Here is the underlined area where: "The Panther Party is an uncompromising party. It faces reality."

(Whereupon the District Attorney presents the second portion of the article to the Defendant.)

DEFENDANT JAMAL: This is Sunday morning, January 4th, 1970, the *Philadelphia Inquirer.* It's a picture of Wes Cook, Communications Secretary for the Philadelphia Chapter, Black Panther Party.

BY MR. McGILL:

Q. Is that you?

A. That was my name when I was born.

Q. Well, is that you in that picture?

A. That is a picture of me twelve years ago. It says: "This organization is doing what the churches are supposed to do. Chapter office is at 1928 Columbia Ave."

"Protest killings by police. Headquarters cold, but issues are hot for Black Panthers. By Acel Moore of the *Inquirer* Staff."

"The walls in the storefront headquarters at 1928 Columbia Ave. are painted black and plastered with revolutionary posters. The faces are dark and determined. Black men and women bundled in coats and jackets against the cold of the unheated interior are busy with telephones, paperwork, or huddling in earnest conferences and barely take time to acknowledge new arrivals or departures. When they do, the standard salutation is a slogan, 'All power to the people'."

180

"It was busy before at the Philadelphia Chapter Head-quarters of the Black Panther Party. It's busier now."

" 'Since the murders,' says Wes Cook, Chapter Communications Secretary, 'Black brothers and sisters and organizations which wouldn't commit themselves before are relating to us. Black people are facing the reality that the Black Panther Party has been facing: political power grows out of the barrel of a gun'."

Q.   So that is a quote, isn't it?

A.   "Political power grows out of the barrel of a gun."

Q.   Mr. Jamal, is that a quote or is it not?

A.   Can I finish reading?

Q.   Well, is it a quote or isn't it?

A.   Can I finish reading it?

Q.   Well, will you answer the question?

A.   Didn't I ask if I could read this in its entirety?

Q.   Will you anwer the question? Are there quotation marks there?

MR. JACKSON: Your Honor—Your Honor—Your Honor —

A.   Will you stop interrupting me?

MR. JACKSON: He already agreed to let him read it. May he read it?

A. If you want to go over it after I finish, that's okay.

MR. McGILL: Would Your Honor rule?

THE COURT: Let him read it.

MR. McGILL: Okay.

DEFENDANT JAMAL: " 'Since the murders'," says Wes Cook, Chapter Communication Secretary, 'Black brothers and sisters and organizations which wouldn't commit themselves before are relating to us. Black people are facing the reality that the Black Panther Party has been facing: political power grows out of the barrel of a gun'."

"Murder's a calculated design of genocide and a national plot to destroy the party leadership is what the Panthers and their supporters call a bloody two-year history of police raids and shootouts. The Panthers say 28 party members have died in police gunfire during that period, two last month."

"Police who have had officers killed and wounded by Panther gunfire deny there is a plot. Police have been shot at, they say, simply and they have shot back."

"Nevertheless, the gun battles and arrests of Panther leaders have convinced the Black Panthers that it is a party under siege."

"Although there have been no shootouts between Philadelphia Panthers and police, Cook—who ranks behind Defense Capt. Reggie Schell and Sister Love, a young woman who is Field Lieutenant in the Philadelphia leadership—says there could have been."

"On September the 28th, the FBI arrested Schell on a charge of possession of a stolen government weapon after alleging finding a loaded Marine M–14 rifle in his room and City Police raided the Party Headquarters confiscating some office equipment."

" 'They would have shot us then,' Cook recently told a visitor to the Headquarters, speaking with deliberate conviction, 'Except we were all out in the community working at the time'."

"There were no visible weapons in the Headquarters, but we can't hope to exist, he said, without some kind of protection."

"Referring frequently to the Party's newspaper, *The Black Panther,* Wes stressed the aim of the Black Panther Party of helping Black Americans gain a sense of dignity and of the Party's insistence on self-defense."

"There are 26 rules outlining the *Black Panther* newspaper for Party members. One of them stipulates that no Party member will use, point or fire a weapon of any kind unnecessarily, or accidentally hurt anyone. Another rule, however, states that all Panthers must learn to operate and service weapons correctly."

" 'Genocide is coming to the forefront under the Nixon, Agnew and Mitchell regime,' says Wes, 'and that's exactly what it is. The Panther Party is an uncompromising Party. It faces reality'."

"In Philadelphia at least the Panthers have been more socially activist than militant. Their rhetoric, frequent references to policemen as 'Facist pigs,' and a 'Racist, Capitalistic American Society,' has been angrier than their actions."

"Like other Panther chapters, the Philadelphia Black Panther Party has established a free breakfast program for needy children. Cook estimates that the Philadelphia Panthers feed about 80 children daily—the number fluctuates some—at two centers, 1916 W. Columbia Avenue and at the Houston Community Center, 8th St. and Snyder Ave."

"Pennsylvania Black Panther Party members have also initiated breakfast programs in Harrisburg and in Reading. The food is obtained primarily from donations by merchants in black ghetto areas, but Cook denies charges which have been made, accusing the Panthers of intimidation. The donations, he said, are voluntary."

BY MR. McGILL:

Q. Mr. Jamal, let me ask you again, sir, if I may—

MR. McGILL: If I may ask a question, Judge. Was that or was that not a quote that you made to Acel Moore?

A. That was a quote from Mao Tse-Tung.

Q. Is that one that you have adopted?

A. Say again?

Q. Have you adopted that as your philosophy theory?

A. No, I have not adopted that. I repeated that.

Q. Let me ask you, Mr. Jamal, when you were before this Court, I believe it was yesterday, you said: "The system is finished." Is that correct?

A. That's correct.

Q. During the course of this trial, several times, sir, you continuously said, "That rulings went one way or the other and they would go against you at times." You would then say, "Rulings are not to my satisfaction," and then, you would go on and on and on and on.

Is that accurate?

A. What did I say, "Going on and on and on?" Are you quoting me now?

Q. Well, did you not continue to complain —

A. What did I say?

Q. —argue and continually —

A. What did I say?

(...)

Q. Mr. Jamal, on April the 29th, 1982, do you recall being in front of Judge Ribner?

A. Yes.

Q. And do you recall over about two or three actual pages of testimony saying such things as—and this was in court, open court—"I don't give a damn what you think, go to hell. What the hell are you afraid of? What the hell are you afraid of, bastard?"

Do you recall saying that to Judge Ribner?

A. Sure do. (Nods head affirmatively.)

MR. McGILL: I have nothing further, Judge.

MR. JACKSON: Mr. Jamal, do you have anything further?

DEFENDANT JAMAL: (Shaking head negatively) No. (Waving of the hand away.)

MR. JACKSON: The defense would rest, Your Honor.

THE COURT: Members of the jury, you must now decide whether the defendant is to be sentenced to death —

MR. JACKSON: Excuse me, Your Honor, may I see you at side-bar?

THE COURT: I'm sorry, I'm sorry.

MR. JACKSON: Yes.

THE COURT: You're right.

MR. JACKSON: May I proceed, Your Honor?

THE COURT: Go ahead.

MR. JACKSON: Ladies and gentlemen, you are, of course, now at the juncture where you must decide whether Mr. Jamal should receive life imprisonment or the imposition of the death penalty....

The Man Malcolm

What you talking 'bout, "down South?"
Long as you south of the Canadian bor-
der, you "down South!"

— *Malcolm X*

Rarely has a name fit its owner so badly as the name bequeathed upon the child, Malcolm, by his forebears.

Malcolm Little was his birth name, but as is common in African and Asian societies, the names given one at birth may no longer fit at life's end.

Malcolm, who in his brief term of years strode across the world's stage, mesmerizing the Black world, electrifying the white, was many things — "Little" was not one of them.

If white America had its way, however, "Little" he would have been, and his impact upon the lives of millions would have been little indeed, if at all.

As a junior high school student in Lansing, Michigan's Mason Jr. High, the tall teen attended a Careers Day Counseling Sessions and confided to one white counselor that he wanted to be a lawyer.

The counselor smirked at the young man's ambition, suggesting he take courses in carpentry, a more "realistic occupation for a nigger."

The intensely sensitive youth smarted at the remark, as if stung, and this crucial point marked his alienation from school, the rural setting of Lansing, and white America.

Denied an education fitted to his quick, natural intellect, he would later gravitate to the grim education of the streets, and begin his swift descent into hell.

"Hell" as in a true, temporal dwelling of torment; no Danteist Inferno of vision and eventual enlightenment, no! Hell, de facto, as in man-made dungeons designed to dehumanize Black life, as in American prisons.

There, at the dawn of his manhood, twenty-one years, after four years of hustling on Harlem's mean New York streets, selling marijuana and committing armed robbery, the man Malcolm, now transformed into 'Detroit Red' (a street sobriquet), would enter America's brutal Bastilles.

So alienated was he in the midst of this dreaded experience that he became further embittered, and fellow inmates tagged the lanky, reddish-brown complexioned convict with the ultimate nickname from the realm of negativity — "Satan."

Confused, angry, bitter, he earned the name and charged the prison air with the promise of malice.

Rejected by a society that never accepted him, locked down in America's uniquely hellish prisons, he was a study in alienation.

His brothers, Wilfred and Philbert, wrote him and sent him tracts from an organization which expounded Black pride and the spiritual superiority of Black folk.

"Satan" was ripe for transformation.

Within months, his sharp mind honed on the extraordinary message coming from this little-known group, the Nation of Islam, Malcolm emerged from behind the satanic mask, and embarked upon a campaign of learning via correspondence courses, studying English and the Romanic root language, Latin.

He devoured books on religion, philosophy, and history.

Due solely to his warrior's will, and his teaching, he emerged from seven years in hell, a sharp, disciplined soldier for the Nation, committed to the millenialist, nationalist movement headed by the NOI Messenger, Elijah Muhammad.

From that day forward, in whatever highway of life he found himself, he would hearken back to his days in the pit, and there find strength for transformation.

He became Malcolm X, and after a painful psychic and organizational split with his aging mentor, became El-Hajj Malik El-Shabazz, following his eye-opening Hajj to the Saudi Arabian city of Mekkah.

Malcolm's life, then, is an intense study in human transformation, from disillusioned youth to hardened criminal, from naive convert to national spokesman, from authentic Afro-American leader to martyr, and from Satan to Sage.

His extraordinary life touched lives globally, causing Africans and Afro-Americans both to react lovingly to a truly remarkable kindred soul.

According to NOI cosmology, American Blacks were descendants of "Asiatics."

Malcolm, almost singlehandedly, utilizing his extraordinary intellect, went beyond the learned myth, and energized a potent reality when he visited African states, dusting off centuries of negative propaganda, thus restoring Mother Africa as the rightful origin of the earth's Black peoples (and, indeed, all people).

His life, and his remarkable personal legacy of human transformation, led directly to the militant era of the Black

Cultural and Political Revolts of the late 1960s and 1970s.

The late Dr. Huey P. Newton, ex-Minister of Defense of the Black Panther Party, drew direct inspiration from Malcolm's challenge that Blacks defend themselves from the racist society.

Dr. Newton often opined that the Panthers were the "Heirs of Malcolm," so vital was his teaching to its world-view.

It is not coincidental that one of the Party's first public armed actions was the assemblage of escorts for Malcolm's widow, Dr. Betty Shabazz, when she visited the Bay Area in the late 1960s.

Malcolm's life, however, must be placed in its proper historical context.

His father, the Rev. Earl Little, was an idealistic "race man," as the term was used at the time, a man Malcolm described as "very, very dark."

Rev. Little was a devotee of the fiery Jamaican orator, journalist, and organizer, Marcus Garvey, and was an organizer of Garvey's Universal Negro Improvement Association, assigned to organize Blacks in Malcolm's home town of Omaha, Nebraska.

Rev. Little's courage in the late 1920s sparked fiery response from the Ku Klux Klan, who burned the Little homestead to the ground.

Young Malcolm's perception, then, of America was its own "nativist" terrorism against Blacks, without official response.

Several years thereafter, Rev. Little's body would be found severed, decapitated, silent tribute to America's response to an uppity Nigger.

Traumatized, bitter to the core, alienated from a culture most foreign, Malcolm's eventual transformation into a whole, loving, integrated human being, takes on all the trappings of miracle.

How many Malcolms sit unripened in today's classrooms throughout urban America, their natural intelligence dulled by a process which fails to teach them?

How many Malcolms cum "Satans" sit stewing in pits of state-designed hatred, imprisoned in soul and in mind?

How many Malcolms, submerged in deadly street life, use their quick minds to compute poisonous profits from crack, instead of contributing their wills and skills to the collective good?

In short, where are today's Malcolms?

In schools, potential untapped.

In prisons, potential entrapped.

In streets, potential sapped.

Malcolm, in his many lives, touched so many because he lived so many lives.

His is a tale of Overcoming.

Malcolm once noted: "History is the best subject to reward our research."

Since his 1965 assassination, the history of Africans in America shows a marked decline in the wellbeing and momentum of the Black masses.

Individual anecdotes of "success" are emblazoned across American media to show a face of Black America patently at odds with reality.

True, Americans elected their first Black governor (a Mulatto millionaire lawyer), but how many major media outlets tell the world that in Virginia, with its 18% Black population, well over 51% of that state's death row was Black, as of November 1987; or that, since 1930, of the 93 persons put to death by the state, 75% plus were Black, many for rape!

If El-Hajj Malik El-Shabazz were alive today, he would

look at the plight of African-Americans today and weep.

What made him so universally loved was his love for everyday, average Black folk, for whence did he come?

It is the malaise, the lack of momentum, the omnipresent feeling of utter aloneness in a wilderness of hostility that marks life for far too many Africans in the U.S.

Malik Shabazz would weep — and then he would work to liberate the many unfound Malcolms rotting in America's schools, streets, and prisons.

No history exists in a vacuum.

Events of centuries, decades, years ago flow like waves through time, to reach our shores of today.

Malcolm truly has meaning when we of this age understand his message of self-defense, as the Panthers did, as MOVE does, today.

> On the Move!
> Long Live John Africa's Revolution!

2/8/90 (Death Row)

Panther Daze Remembered

The four passengers of the dark-colored, two-tone sedan glide over a span of steel-girded bridge in Upper-North Philadelphia. All is dark, save for the blurry stars of headlights passing each other, like meteors, shooting swiftly by.

Suddenly, sharp stabs of blood-red light pierce the dark interior, jarring several men out of nods.

"Awww, shit!!" Stretch glowers, a yawn cutting off angry curses.

A short burst of shrill siren, and a blinding searchlight slices dark irises and bounces painfully off of eight retinas, leaving a garish afterglow shining behind closed lids.

Mary pulls over the ride and two cops appear at each door, barking at occupants harshly.

Four men pile out into the false, electronic day, torn by the throbbing rotating red eye atop the car.

One cop covers, while the younger conducts an abrupt pat search.

"What's this?" he asks, his nervous fingers running over a "suspicious" bulge in my top left-hand jacket pocket.

I am sleepy, ornery, and pissed at this intrusion, at the gall of two rednecks stopping, searching and probably arresting four Black men in the midst of the Black community. I stand, arms outstretched, in scarecrowish silence.

The cop, hooked now, pops the snap, digs his skinny white fingers into the pocket, and snatches out a worn, dog-eared book, with a red plastic cover.

His attention distracted, he flips through pages, back towards the title page, and slowly, painstakingly, tries to read writing on a filmy page.

"Thee... qun... er, quotations of... uh, uh — what's zis — Mayo Teesey — Tongue... ?!?"

It takes a second before it clicks, then, like a flash of lightning — (*Quotations of Mao Tse-Tung!*) — "Jeezus Keerist!!"

"Communists!!!"

The cop drops the book on cold, wet ground, whips out his .38 revolver, and places it to the skull of the nearest Black man — me.

His hand shakes, his skinny white finger clutches trigger, and four Black men are close to death because some young pimply-faced white rookie cop is aghast that he has apparently uncovered a nigger-commie-spy-ring. "Freeze!!!" he shrieks, assuming a double hand combat stance.

(I mean, whatdafuck did he think we were doing — arms held high in a brisk wind? Hanging up clothes? Playin' B-ball?)

My eyes flick to Reg, the Defense Captain, as I search for direction.

Hot sweat drips down cold flesh, my underarms watering my sides.

Reg looks back with the wisdom of a thousand such street searches — and his dark, slanted eyes shoot upwards, as in "Whatta fuck is this nut tryna prove?"

He glances at the other cop, older, heavier, more senior, and cracks up in whinny-ish horse laughter.

Tension flows from us all as we erupt in laughter, and the

rookie, not knowing the butt of the joke, but beginning to suspect it is himself, steps back a pace, and glances at his elder partner for direction.

He, too, looks skyward, then cuts tired blue eyes toward his well-intentioned, but utterly melodramatic junior partner, smirks, walks over to the wind-blown pages of the red book, picks it up, slides it into my pocket.

We stand silent in wintry night, wind whips thru Afros and denim jackets, arms stretched out and upwards, like dark leafless trees.

The elder whispers to the unbearded youth, a few checks on car radio, a mumbled "routine traffic check," and they depart, in silence.

Two cops had the Defense Captain, Lt. of Security, Lt. of Finance, and Lt. of Information of the Phila. Chapter of the Black Panther Party, the city's chapter leadership, under the gun, and let us go.

We sat back in the car, and laughed anew, at the relief and the loss of tension — how close.

In microcosm, it showed one of the primal reasons for the vast appeal of the BPP.

For, at base, this event, so utterly common and mundane, reflects the lack of autonomy at work in Black communities, where an outsider, a cop, can enter and impose his biased notions upon another.

It is not, nor has ever been, a question of "Law."

It is, and always has been, a matter of "Power."

The power of white America's power structure to impose its will, its biases, its mythologies, its twisted political structures and warped economic system, of gross exploitative consumption, upon another people.

Huey P. Newton, a man of startling, uncommon brilliance, of course, saw this, and, in large part, this very insight fuelled his drive to establish and create a Black revolutionary political party for self-defense.

For, when one considers the prior circumstances on the bridge, what would've happened were we not under the wise, mature leadership of Capt. Reggie Schell?

Or, worse, what if the idiot rookie was paired with another idiot rookie, who was pumped up by the other guy's macho idiocy?

We knew, like too many Black men know in America, later, as we sat in the car, as it rocked with laughter, that we walked in the shadow of death, that we all stand, perpetually, on the crumbling brink of the abyss, on the razor's edge of catastrophe.

Remember Lil' Bobby Hutton; Fred Hampton and Mark Clark; Denzil Dowell; Mike Stewart; MOVE — May 13th; Eleanor Bumpers, and the dark list grows, like a spreading pool of blood, day by day.

To whom could Black youth appeal for our personal autonomy?

To whom could we petition for our personal safety to live, to walk, to ride, to be, in peace?

The Politicians?

The Police?

The Preachers?

In the end, we appealed, logically, to ourselves, and through Huey's doing, this appeal hit the gut, toughing a people too long used to apathy, awakening and energizing us, and bringing the Black Panther Party into being.

Many folks have heard or read of the BPP — but how many remember its first name?

The Black Panther Party for Self-Defense.

Even though the Party later dropped that part, the reasons

remained. Blacks united and armed for self-defense would pose no problems for a people who harbor no ill will towards them, for self-defense is, at base, a human right, in fact, a right of any living species.

But for US "Security" forces, long-accustomed to wreaking havoc on Black life, such a body presented the incipient threat of armed resistance, and reprisal.

For America's white police forces, this meant an end to the free ride — no longer could the forces of the empire inflict pain and loss upon a people without a militant response.

Huey's determined, principled stance, overnite, created a psychic umbrella of protection over America's Black community, as the one fundamental right that all life shares, the singular principle of self-defense, seeped, like Spring rain after a desert drought, into the awakened consciousness of a parched people to whom this basic law was denied.

Like dark roses, BPP offices sprouted across America in response to this fresh, new wind.

Consider, if you will, the horizon before us twenty, almost thirty, years after the Panthers' birth, and its cruel poisoning by the state's agents of COINTELPRO.

Today, the Panther lies slain, its principles, its weapons, lying in the gutter, rusty from non-use.

Today, our communities are virtual deserts of drug infestation, with no broad-based, independent Black political self-defense body in place, and our people are, once again, victims of a wave of state terrorism.

What does it matter that Black police chiefs, or for that matter Black mayors, sit at the helms of power, if Black life is cheaper, and white cops still wipe out Black life with utter impunity?

Huey P. Newton organized a revolutionary political party

to give expression to Black will for personal, political, and national autonomy, so that our lives, our ideas, and our people could be respected.

He took the struggle for Black liberation farther, deeper than any of his contemporaries.

He presided over the founding of the Party's First Intercommunal Headquarters, a de facto First Afro-American People's Embassy on North African soil, in independent, revolutionary Algeria, a haven, a home of independent Black revolutionary thought.

Thanks to Huey's remarkable, radical vision, Africans from America returned to our Ancient Motherland, not like the "Founders" of Liberia, to expand the U.S. Empire; nor like former U.S. envoy to South Africa, Mr. Perkins, in the employ of the ruling class, but free, able and willing to link up with the world's liberation movements, to rebel against the oppression visited upon Black life daily, to build revolution.

But the system, as it must do to survive, counter-attacked by placing Black faces in high places, by cosmetic reform.

Black cops swelled inner city ranks.

Black legislators went to Washington and state capitals.

Black jurists ascended to previously lily-white benches.

To what avail, twenty, twenty-five years later?

Black cops enforce ruling class, white laws, passed by increasingly bourgeois Black legislators, decided by Black jurists who merely mimic the hoary precedents of white, ruling class privilege. The same legacy of oppression that demeaned and devalued the blood, sweat, and tears of our fathers.

Huey knew we had to take the big step, the final, irrevocable, truly historic breach away from this system, to revolution.

We walked to the edge, tiptoed to the brink, and backed away.

Our people, the poor, everyday Black folks from whom we come, have been catching hell ever since.

Blinded by the lying illusion of reform, we believed things were getting better.

"We movin' on up"... Yeah, like the Jeffersons, actors reading lines.

Meanwhile, our streets are crammed with homeless, the jails are swelled with Black youth; our lives cheapen by the day, and all this system offers is an Iron Fist, or the 1990s illusion — "The Cosby Show."

Black grandmothers, like Eleanor Bumpers, are slain in our homes by white, triggerhappy racist cops. Black babies, like the MOVE kids, are bombed into infinity—by white racist cops.

Black girls, like Tawana Brawley, are brutally raped and degraded — by white racist cops, and then re-raped by racist swine on white grand juries, selected by racist, ambitious DAs, presided over by white blind judges, and told to us by a media just as white, just as racist, just as vividly anti-African, as the cops who committed the first foul deed.

Ex-Black Panthers, like Geronimo Pratt (L.A. Chapter); Ed Poindexter, David Rice, Dharuba Moore, Delbert Africa, and others remain shackled in this beast's cancerous bowels, prisoners of a system that provides not even a shadow of fairness, nor due process, for those who dared rise up against this monster.

Into this dark, cold night, a point of brilliant light was poised to shine once more—the active return of Huey P. Newton, to the struggle.

In his last published interview with the Black 'Frisco

paper, *The Sun Reporter,* Huey was quoted as saying:

"With Nixon and George Bush having dumped so many drugs in the Black community, the community is in disarray and fragmented. The street gangs have kept the community divided.

"It is difficult to organize a community under these circumstances.

"The drug situation keeps the ability to organize at a standstill.

"The influx of drugs into the Black community is designed to destroy progressive organizations... I believe that self-determination in Black communities will give us control over all institutions in our community."

Poised on the brink of re-entering the fray, this bold and brilliant warrior was struck down — worse, struck down by a Black hand — a hand he had fed, a youth he had nurtured — a youth a stranger to himself, lost and turned out by that demon — crack.

What would Huey have said, in his own memory, his life of positivity snuffed out by negative, mindless energy?

Huey once asked, "Prison, where is thy sting? Death, where is thy victory?"

For us to go back into our lives of quietude grants death a victory in Huey's life that it does not deserve.

We prevail over death when we remember our fallen and when we continue the march.

We must remember the wonder that formed his brilliant mind, the love that animated that great heart, the impish joy that fed his glowing smile, and yes, the demons that dogged his later years — yes! For Huey, like us, was not a perfect being; he was, above all, a man of determined purpose, and even with his moral flaws, a man who stood, head 'n shoulders, above the rest.

Such a memory is mightier than death.

From the faded pages of the Red Book comes Mao's observation, still correct after all these years, that death comes to us all in different forms.

Death, Mao reasoned, could be "lighter than a feather" or "heavier than Mount Tai."

Huey's demise does not diminish the splendid example he set in his extraordinary life of service to the revolutionary aspirations of an oppressed people — for that alone, the name Huey P. Newton shines in the ears of the people, a bright shine of love.

While Black stooges and politicians called him "criminal" and "drug addict," everyday Blackfolk laid flowers where he fell.

Those same apologists for this system, when they, like all men, die, will find death "lighter than a feather," for they are a dime a dozen.

Huey's death, because of his matchless courage, mighty love, and stellar brilliance, rocked us all, for his death, as in the death of all truly great men, was, for we who survived him, "heavier than Mt. Tai."

Remember: "All Power to the People Who Believe in Self-Defense!"

On the Move! Long Live John Africa's Revolution and Down with this Rotten Ass System!

10/2/89 Death Row

Assata Shakur

... Mondo Langa

Ruchell Cinque Magee

Abdul Majid

Jalil A. Muntaqin

Sekou Odinga

William O'Neal (in exile)

Hugo Pinell

Geronimo ji-Jaga Pratt

Assata Shakur (in exile)

Mutulu Shakur

Kazi Touré (released)

William Turk / Sekou Kambui

Gary Tyler

Sababu Na Uhuru

Albert Nuh Washington ...

(A partial listing of Black and New Afrikan Political Prisoners and P.O.W.s in the United States)

Prisoner in the United States

Assata Shakur: On the night of May 2, I was shot twice by the New Jersey State Police. I was kept on the floor, kicked, pulled, dragged along by my hair. Finally, I was put into an ambulance, but the police would not let the ambulance leave. They kept asking the ambulance attendant: "Is she dead yet? Is she dead yet?" Finally, when it was clear that I wasn't going to die in the next five or ten minutes, they took me to the hospital. The police were jumping on me, beating me, choking me, doing everything that they could possibly do as soon as the doctors or the nurses would go outside. I was half dead—hospital authorities had brought in a priest to give me the last rites—but the police would not stop torturing me. That went on until the next morning, when I was taken to the intensive care unit. They had to calm down a little while I was there. Then they moved me to another room, which was the

---

This is the testimony of Assata Shakur, formerly JoAnne Chesimard Malik, who was arrested on the evening of May 2, 1973, along with Sundiata Acoli and Zayd Malik Shakur (who was killed by the New Jersey state police). Assata Shakur, who is now in exile, in Cuba, was a member of the Black Panther Party and of the Black Liberation Army. Here she gives testimony regarding her treatment after being captured by New Jersey state troopers.

Johnson Suite, and they closed off the exit from the hallway. So they could virtually control all traffic in and out. It was just open season on me for about three or four days. They'd turned up the air conditioning so that I was freezing to death. My lungs were threatening to collapse. They were doing everything so that I would get pneumonia.

Q: Did the medical staff participate or acquiesce to this treatment while you were under their care?

AS: Some of them did. The first night there was a doctor who was just as bad as the state troopers. He said: "Why did you shoot the trooper?"— He didn't know if I had done it or not, but he just jumped on me. Some of the nurses were very supportive; they could really see the viciousness of the police. One of them gave me a call button, so that I could call whenever the state troopers came in my bed. That way I was able to avoid being further beaten up. They had my legs cuffed to the bed, even though I was half dead and my leg was swollen. Some of the nurses protested the way they had my foot cuffed. It was really bleeding and sticking in the flesh.

Q: Is it your opinion that were it not for the medical staff, the police authorities would have murdered you in the hospital with the complicity and compliance of certain doctors.

AS: That's definitely a possibility.

Q: These members of the medical staff that showed human compassion towards you, were they Black or white, or both?

AS: Black and white. The one who gave me the call button was a German nurse; she had a German accent. Some of the Black nurses sent me a little package of books which really saved my life, because that was one of the most difficult times. One was a book of Black poetry, the other was *Siddhartha* by Hermann Hesse, then a book about Black women in white America. It was like the most wonderful selection that they could have possibly given me. They gave me the poetry of our people, the tradition of our women, the relationship of human beings to nature and the search of human beings for freedom, for justice, for a world that isn't a brutal world. And those books—even through that experience—kind of just chilled me out, let me be in touch with my tradition, the beauty of my people, even though we've had to suffer such vicious oppression. Those people in that hospital didn't know who I was, but they understood what was happening to me; and it makes you think that no matter how brutal the police, the courts are, the people fight to keep their humanity, and can really see beyond that.

Q: How long were you at the hospital and how long did your state of medical deterioration last after your capture?

AS: I spent about two weeks at the Middlesex County Hospital. And then I spent another two weeks in the Roosevelt Hospital for the chronically ill. I had two bullet wounds—I still have one bullet in my chest. I was paralyzed in this arm. I had trouble breathing. And after I was released from the second hospital, it took me a couple of years to gain full use of my hand. I was not allowed physical therapy, or medical treatment in the hospital, we had to get a court order for simple things like a rubber ball so I could squeeze my hand and teach myself how to use it again. And the only kind of exercise that I was able to acquire was at the instructions of the nurses. I asked them, what can I do? I was acutely aware that the prison system would do everything possible to frustrate my getting well again. The nurses would give me a towel and even though I couldn't wring it up, they'd say: "Just try." So I would put my hand on top of it—and then the police would come and take the towel away, even though I was cuffed to the bed. I don't know what they thought I was going to do with the towel, but the towel wasn't the point. The point was to just do everything possible to make me suffer.

Q: So is your experience that you were not given any recuperative or rehabilitative therapy for the wounds that you suffered on May 2, 1973?

AS: I was given some, but I mean the state, the police, the DA's office, the FBI, I believe, did everything possible to frustrate my recovery.

Q: So you had to get medical therapy as a consequence of legal litigation.

AS: My lawyers went to court and said, she has one arm that's paralyzed, but I never got physical therapy. We were able to get one team to come in and examine me on one occasion, that was it. The prison doctor would just take my arm and say: 'Oh, it's perfectly fine. You don't have a problem.' And his treatment for most things was laxatives.

Q: After the hospitalization came to an end, were you taken to a detention center or a prison?

AS: Yeah, I was taken to the Middlesex County workhouse. I was put in solitary. A cell which had a door of bars and outside was another big metal door. I was there from June until October–November, when I was taken to the Middlesex County Jail in New Brunswick, and put into a basement, in solitary again. It was a men's jail, and I was the only woman there. I was kept there until I was taken to New York to go on trial in December, 1973.

Q: You were confined to your cell approximately how many hours a day?

AS: Twenty-four hours a day.

Q: Were you allowed contact visits?

AS: The rules were that you could have contact visits with immediate family and lawyers, but the police kept entering our conversations. They would just ignore the fact that there were supposed to be client–lawyer privileges, or that it was a family visit. They would just be there and nothing we could do about it. Children were not even allowed to visit that prison and it was real sad. You'd just hear the children during the visiting hours screaming their parents' names, and they would be outside of the prison. You'd just hear these little voices, it was real painful.

Q: Were you aware at the time that there is a law in the U.S. that says that attorneys and clients have a right to confidentiality?

AS: Yeah. My lawyer (and aunt) Evelyn constantly protested the conditions, but she was talking to deaf ears. She went to court I don't know how many times to have the lawyer–attorney visits respected, with the doors shut, but they were virtually in the room, and that room was bugged any-way.

Q: What do you mean by the term 'bugged'?

AS: I mean that they had electronic listening devices where we would meet. The guards would come around and say: "We know what you're saying." It was their way of saying: "We've got it on tape anyway. So what?"

Q: In your view, did the combination of inadequate medical therapeutic attention and the lack of confidentiality with your attorney impede your ability to defend yourself against the many state charges that were subsequently brought against you?

AS: Absolutely. My lawyers had to fight for such elementary things that they couldn't even deal with the case. The state resisted everything. Most of the energies they would normally be spending preparing for trial, they had to spend filing suits around the right for me to have a ball, to have medical attention, or even have food, which was the worst of any prison that I've ever been in. The women protested the food, it wasn't just me that they brought this food to, but they said that I was the cause of the protest, even though I was held in solitary confinement and could only speak to the women if I climbed up to the top of the bars and talked out of these little holes. Our whole attempt to prepare for the trial was frustrated on every level.

Q: Did you suffer any disciplinary procedures as a consequence of that protest?

AS: I was already in solitary, so the only thing they could do was just harrass me, make my life more difficult.

Q: Did the other women suffer any disciplinary procedure as a consequence of trying to communicate with you?

AS: They were threatened in terms of their court cases; they were told that I was a terrorist ... I was accused of killing a New Jersey state trooper and the police claimed that they had to keep me in solitary for my own protection. But the women didn't believe that. They did every little thing they could to make me feel human.

Q: Could you tell us exactly what happened when you first went to court in your first trial? What were the charges that were brought against you and exactly how did the state deal with prosecuting you in this particular case?

AS: The first trial that I participated in was the New Jersey trial. They put in a whole lot of other charges like armed robbery — I was supposed to have robbed the police of guns — and then assault, and a whole list of charges. But the main charges were murder of a New Jersey state policeman and wounding another one. We were on trial, we were in the jury selecting process.

Q: When you say "we," could you state exactly who —

AS: Sundiata Acoli and I were on trial together. We had the same charges and we decided that we would go on trial together. They didn't oppose that.

Q: Had you recovered from your wounds at the time?

AS: I was still wearing a brace for the broken clavicle, but the problem was mainly my right arm. I was basically paralyzed. And I was a wreck. I'd broken out in a rash, I was very thin... Anyway, we started the jury selection process. And in the middle of it the trial was stopped. It was postponed until January, 1974.

Q: Why?

AS: Because it was found out that there was such a racist climate in the jury room that the trial could no longer proceed. There was like this lynch mob atmosphere, there was no way we could receive anything resembling a fair trial. So they gave us a change of venue to another county—Morris County—where we were supposed to resume the trial. Morris County happened to be 99 % white and one of the richest counties in the state of New Jersey, as a matter of fact, in the whole country.

Q: What evidence was presented to indicate that there was a racist climate at that time?

AS: There was no evidence presented, but the press had been trying me for years. I was turned into a monster. They pictured this vicious woman that goes around terrorizing police, this madwoman essentially... They had created this whole mythology in order to destroy me. They started building this whole campaign in the press in 1970–71. The press were free to say anything and the police, the FBI, the CIA were the ones who were feeding the press information. No one ever asked me any questions or even attempted to deal with the fact that we were human beings, people who had a long history of struggle. It was just overwhelming, and people believed that.

Q: You notice that there was a correlation between the information the police had in their possession and the information and the distortions in the press?

AS: It wasn't information. They just fabricated things, and fed them to the press. They would accuse me of having I don't know how many pending charges, and none of that was true. Anybody reading the paper would think that we had been convicted of commiting so many crimes all around the country and never was there a mention that we'd never been found guilty of any crime.

Q: You said that the trial was suspended because you could not get an impartial jury panel. Did you have the opportunity to select a jury of your peers when the trial was recommenced?

AS: No. The jury selecting process was biased. Most of the Blacks who were prospective jurists were gotten rid of by the prosecution. Then, people who obviously were prejudiced, and obviously thought that I was guilty, were included in the jury. At the second trial in New Jersey there was a severance and I went to trial alone. The judge would say: "Well, can you put your opinion aside? Can you follow the law as I give it to you? Can you listen to my instructions and come to a verdict?" Even though a poll was taken that showed that 70% of the people of Middlesex County believed that I was guilty and had heard of the case through the media, the judge said it was a fair trial and there was no prejudice. I was tried and convicted by an all-white jury, a jury that was clearly prejudiced in favor of the prosecution. The jury was sequestered but the police and the jurors kept intermingling freely. The same thing happened in Sundiata's case. One of the black jurors in his case tried to really come forth but they beat her down. There was a real investigation of the way in which the police interacted with the guards, the court officers interacted with jurors while they were sequestered, and especially in cases where the defendant is charged with the killing of a police officer, that's a tool of influencing the jury.

Q: In December of 1978 your attorney, along with other organizations and groups, filed a petition in the UN Commission on Human Rights, alleging a consistent pattern of gross violations of human rights in regard to prisoners in the U.S. Your case was one of those that were cited, and you were visited by a group of international jurists and attorneys. Could you tell us exactly what type of unit you were housed in and for how long and under what conditions?

AS: Well, I spent two and a half years—maybe more—in these prisons. After I was convicted in 1977 I was taken to Quentin prison for women for about a week, and after that I was transferred to Yardsville, which is an all-men's prison. Not a jail, a prison. They gave me a booklet: "These are the rules for the New Women's Unit at Yardsville Prison." I was the only woman in the New Women's Unit and they told me that I was going to be there for the rest of my life. They got a prison psychologist to testify that I was a hardened revolutionary and that no amount of time in solitary confinement would bother my mental health whatsoever. I was kept in this—it was like a cage—within a completely isolated section of the prison. There were two guards in front of the cell at all times, lights at all times.

Q: Were these female guards?

AS: No. Male and female guards. In front of my cell, writing down everything, you know: 'Subject is now eating. Subject is now on the toilet. Subject is now reading'—everything I did they wrote. I had no contact with the other prisoners, no access to the legal library, no access to any of the other educational facilities, no outside recreation whatsoever. No—my family visits were held in a filthy, nasty place—a search room for the normal prisoners. And so we had to sit in this filthy—and it was just unbearably filthy—room and have our visits, what few visits I was permitted to have. Lawyers' visits also took place in that room. The other thing I talked about to the international lawyers was the fact that I had been sent to Alderson, West Virginia, which is a prison within a prison. Although I had no federal charges, there's this agreement called the Interstate Contact Agreement, by which any person in order to settle their relationships with their family, with their community, can be shipped into the federal prison system anywhere in the country. Sundiata was sent to Marion prison, which is the worst concentration camp in the United States. Alderson was set up for the most "dangerous" women in the U.S., a maximum of 20. Two of them were Manson family women, one had been accused of attempted assault against President Ford, and the rest of the women—the overwhelming majority—were members of the Aryan Sisterhood, which is a fascist, Nazi organization. Even though the prisoner population in Alderson in general is overwhelmingly Black—Black, Latino, Asian—the control unit was all white, with the exception of me. I was there with thirteen or fifteen Nazis who wore swastikas embroidered on their jeans, who took pictures giving Hitler salutes. And I was there until the unit was closed down and I was shipped into the Hole...

Q: What is the Hole?

AS: The Hole is solitary confinement. It's punitive segregation. Even though I had not been accused of any disciplinary infraction the whole time that I was there, I was thrown into the Hole while they were deciding what to do with me. They didn't want me to be in the prison population, in any normal situation, so I had to stay in the Hole until they finally decided that they were going to ship me back to Quentin Prison. In Quentin Prison, immediately on my arrival, they closed the building that I was in, which meant that all of the women who worked in the prison, and were going to school or had jobs in the population lost their jobs and could only move around inside of the maximum security building. All of the recreation programs women had been allowed to participate in—until I came—they lost all of that. And the prison administration would go around to the women, saying: "She's the reason that you've lost your job and are no longer able to get an education. She's the reason why you are confined to this building 24 hours a day." I could see that prison officials were trying to create a situation where the women would move on me. They had moved most of the women who had some kind of an insight as to what was going on to the other maximum security building, and had crowded the building where I was with women who were informers, who were tools of the administrations or women who were just mad or who were absolute fools.

Q: So is it your view that the prison authorities tried to incline other inmates to physically attack you?

AS: Oh yes. They would incite these women constantly; they had their people moved to that building especially for

that purpose, women who had no long-term sentences, no reason to be in that building, were sent there for the sole purpose
of stirring up trouble. It got to the point where guards—Black
guards—would say: "Don't go outside today 'cause they got
something cooked up for you." I would always listen to what
the guards had to say with a grain of salt, but in certain
instances I found out that they were saying the truth.

Q: According to the United States Constitution, everyone
accused of a crime has the right to choose their own attorney,
and if they do not have the funds to choose or to afford the
attorney of their choice, they are then appointed an attorney
by the court. This is the law of the land. The records reflect in
your case, however, that one of your attorneys was mysteriously killed during the course of one of your trials. Could you
explain to us the trial that you were attending, what happened,
and what is known about that, how that impacted your ability
to defend yourself?

AS: This happened in trial in Jersey. There was a consistent attack on my lawyers. They were being threatened with
contempt, with being thrown off the case—that's the first
thing. Stanley Cohen, who was murdered, was one of the
lawyers on that case. There is a myth that someone who's
accused of a crime has a right to a lawyer. The reality of it is
that most people who have no money get lawyers who have
no interest in their case, do no investigation, no work whatsoever. In my case, the state had millions of dollars at their com-
mand to prosecute me and we had no money whatsoever. We
needed experts to mount a defense, ballistics experts, because
so much of the evidence—the so-called physical evidence—
was manufactured. Things that appeared on discovery reports
then disappeared, then appeared again, and it was obvious that

all the evidence was tampered with. So we needed a forensic chemist, an investigator, ballistics experts, and we had absolutely no money. Finally, after the lawyers whooped and hollered, the judge gave an order granting some assistance in paying for the experts, even though it's very difficult to find a ballistics expert or a forensic expert who doesn't work for the police, especially if you're being accused of murdering a police officer. Just finding one was a task in and of itself. Stanley Cohen had made some initial contacts and initial agreements with an investigator, and was en route to being able to deal with some of these experts and expose some of this tampered evidence—and the next thing I knew, he was found dead in his apartment. The cause of his death has never been made public. The initial report said that he was a victim of trauma—but we never got the real cause of death, whether or not he was murdered. They finally said something about natural causes, but there never was a report of how he was killed. What we do know was that all of my legal records that were in his apartment were taken by the United States—no, by the New York Police Department—everything. They said that they took those—my legal records—as evidence. They didn't say evidence of what. Evelyn had to file a lawsuit to get those legal records back. Different records were missing; all the notes that referred to investigations of the case were never found. Then, immediately after Stanley Cohen's death, the judge retracted the orders saying that the state had to help us pay for these experts. The city's order said that we hadn't gotten these experts in time, and therefore the order was no longer good. William Kunstler was one of the lawyers on the case, and so was Lennox Hines; the next thing we knew, both of them were cited for contempt. The judge held a hearing to get Kunstler thrown off the case, because he was trying to raise money so we could pay the experts. Instead of even being able to prepare my defense, my lawyers were put in a position where they had to prepare their own defenses... And that went on through my whole time in prison. Evelyn Williams—who was also my aunt—was my lawyer. She was cited for contempt, she was smitten with it daily, she spent time in prison for contempt, for no reason at all. That happened to most of my lawyers, if not all of them: they were all threatened. Lou Meyers, a lawyer from Mississippi, said that he would rather try a million cases in Mississippi than try one in New Jersey, because New Jersey was the most racist place he'd ever been in. But it wasn't just New Jersey, it was New York, it was every place that I went to trial in. And it didn't happen just to me; this was something that was repeated across the board in all cases that concerned political prisoners; on every single case the lawyers were harassed, the prisoners received the worst treatment.

Q: Was your family in any way harassed or intimidated by state authorities during this whole period?

AS: Absolutely. First, let me say that the prison authorities try to make the visits as uncomfortable as possible. They build prisons in places where it's very hard to visit. Families have to spend hours in line, just waiting to get in, standing out in the cold. There are no facilities for them, often nothing to drink. When my daughter was tiny, my mother would bring her to visit me, and the guards would say: "She can't have milk. She can't have diapers." Just insane things to make life so much more difficult. My family was subjected to police harassment on every level. My mother had a heart attack because the police went to her job, they tried to storm the door. Surveillance cameras, phone bugs, devices, strange phone calls at all hours of the night playing forged recordings of my voice, all this stuff they suffered because they were my family. They couldn't just sit and have a conversation in the house, everything was being recorded. Part of the car's motor would fall off and then they would take it to the garage and see that it had been mysteriously sawed; tires would be slashed. Letters, all kinds of letters, from police agents, threatening letters—it was just an onslaught of harassment, meant to break them down and destroy our family unity, trying to turn us against each other, trying to scare them to death so that they would be afraid even to have a relationship with me. But it didn't work. We survived it, and I think that our family is stronger as a result of that. We resisted together, and we struggled together, and that has made us—all of us—much more serious about who we are and about our love for each other.

Chronology of the Black Panther Party

1965

February 21 El-Hajj Malik El-Shabazz (Malcolm X) slain in New York City.

1966

Fall Huey Newton and Bobby Seale meet at Merritt Community College in Oakland, California, where Huey's brother Melvin is a sociology professor. The best read and most outspoken campus activist, Newton develops a reputation as a serious Black nationalist leader. Both Newton and Seale believe that the Black student activities on campus should be more related to the Black community.

October Working in a local poverty program, Huey and Bobby begin to canvass the Black community of Oakland to ascertain the needs and desires of the people. They formulate the *Ten-Point Program and Platform—What We*

---

*This chronology was taken in part from the February 1991 issue of **The Black Panther**, Black Community News Service and from a thesis paper by Kit Holder.*

1966, continued

Want, What We Believe. Copies are distributed throughout Oakland. The Black Panther Party for Self-Defense (BPP) is officially formed.

October-November Huey Newton, Minister of Defense; Bobby Seale, Chairman; and Bobby Hutton, Treasurer (17-year-old recruit from local poverty program) raise money by selling *The Red Book, Quotations from Chairman Mao,* and Frantz Fanon's *The Wretched of the Earth.* With the proceeds they buy guns and print up literature.

November The BPP establishes patrols to monitor Oakland police activities within the Black community. With law books, various guns, and a few cars, founding members drive around Oakland watching the police and advising Black people of their legal rights. A pre-law student, Huey Newton had researched the California laws concerning the public display of arms and interference with police activities. He is on probation for a minor encounter with the police and is not legally eligible to carry a handgun. Thus, he carries a shotgun. Bobby Hutton, who is underage, also does not qualify to possess a handgun. Bobby Seale carries a .45 caliber automatic pistol in a shoulder holster worn over his jacket. In the act of advising people of their rights or confronting the police, the Panthers stand at the legal distance from the police and the "suspect."

1967

January BPP for Self-Defense opens storefront office in Oakland, holds meetings and political education classes as well as rallies around their *Ten-Point Program and Platform,* particularly point #7: "We want an immediate end to Police Brutality and Murder of Black People."

February 21 Betty Shabazz, widow of El-Hajj Malik El-Shabazz (Malcolm X), visits San Francisco Bay Area. BPP for Self-Defense responsible for her security. They are confronted by police, who want to disarm them, at the airport —and outside the offices of *Ramparts* magazine. They are legally exercising their constitutional right to bear arms, and no arrests are made. These incidents are widely publicized in Northern California.

April 27 The first issue of *The Black Panther,* Black Community News Service, is published. A four-page mimeographed newspaper, the issue is headlined: "Why Was Denzil Dowell Killed," and deals extensively with the police murder of an innocent, unarmed Black youth in Richmond, California. BPP organizes the community in protest to this killing, and gains more support for its police patrols.

March—May BPP works with community on other issues, such as installing stop signs at dangerous intersections, and a community review board for the police department. Panther patrol cars are frequently stopped by police.

May BPP chapter formed in Jersey City, NJ.

May 21 Gun-carrying BPP members and supporters demonstrate at the State Capitol in Sacramento on the Constitutional right to bear arms. In response to a proposed bill to restrict this right, the BPP issues Executive Mandate #1 on the Capitol steps. The document, written by Newton is entitled "In Defense of Self-Defense."

May Eldridge Cleaver joins the Panthers as Minister of Information. BPP officially terminates its police patrols in Oakland before impending bill is passed.

June 29 Stokely Carmichael, a leader of the well-known Student Non-Violent Coordinating Committee (SNCC), is drafted into the BPP, with rank of Field Marshall.

1967 continued

August 25 A classified FBI memo circulated to all Bureau field offices (41 nationwide) details plans to "disrupt, misdirect, discredit or otherwise neutralize" Black liberation movement groups.

October BPP office opened in Newark, NJ.

October 28 Driving through Oakland late at night, Huey Newton is stopped by two police officers. A shoot-out ensues: Officer John Frey is shot and killed, Newton and Officer Herbert Heans seriously wounded. Newton is arrested for murder, assault, and attempted murder although he claimed he had passed out and did not know who shot the police. No gun was found on Newton.

November Kathleen Cleaver from SNCC moves to San Francisco and works with BPP newspaper. "Free Huey" campaign begins with mass rallies, SNCC-inspired pickets, paramilitary marches outside courthouse. BPP membership grows to over 200. Noted San Francisco lawyer Charles R. Garry becomes Newton's attorney.

December 8 Bobby Seale released from jail (from Sacramento incident).

December Seale and Eldridge Cleaver speak nationwide on behalf of Huey Newton.

December 22 BPP develops a coalition with the Peace and Freedom Party (PFP), a mainly white liberal/progressive political party which runs candidates in local and national elections. Eventually Eldridge Cleaver ran for president on the PFP ticket, Seale and Newton for local office in the name of the *Ten-Point Program and Platform* and Kathleen Cleaver for local office in San Francisco.

1968

January Alprentice "Bunchy" Carter and Earl Anthony help form Southern California branch of Black Panther Party. Tactical police break into Eldridge and Kathleen Cleaver's apartment looking for guns, in vain.

February 17–18 Two major "Free Huey" rallies are held, one in Oakland and one in L.A. SNCC leaders James Forman, H. Rap Brown and Stokely Carmichael are each given nominal positions in the BPP in order to avoid favoring any possible SNCC factions.

February Police break into Bobby Seale's house and arrest him and his wife Artie, charging both with illegal possession of a sawed-off shotgun. The gun turned out to have neither Bobby's nor Artie's fingerprints on it. Police also charge Bobby Seale with "conspiracy to commit murder," claiming they heard him say: "We should get Rap." Seale states this was an attempt by police to cause friction within SNCC, and between SNCC and the BPP, which he was carefully trying to prevent.

March Seattle Chapter of BPP opens. Kansas City BPP office raided. Five Panthers arrested. BPP issues Executive Mandate #3, which calls for all BPP members to legally arm and defend themselves. Arthur Morris, brother of "Bunchy" Carter is shot and killed by agents of the U.S. government. Both Cleaver and Seale receive rumors, one from a Black former Oakland police officer, that the police are planning an action against the BPP for April.

March 4 Secret FBI memo directs Bureau offices to "prevent the coalition of militant Black nationalist groups... prevent the rise of a Black 'Messiah' who would unify and electrify the Black nationalist movement."

April 3 Shotgun-weilding Oakland police break into a BPP

1968 *continued*

meeting at St. Augustine's Church in West Oakland.

April 4 Martin Luther King, Jr. is slain. Bobby Seale urges Oakland Black community to refrain from rioting, but to organize and defend their community. Oakland does not riot; however, many people approach the BPP for guns.

April 6 At night, after final preparations for a massive "Free Huey" and election campaign barbecue/picnic in Oakland, a carload of BPP members is ambushed by police on a side street. Police begin a two-hour shoot-out which ends with Bobby Hutton, after surrendering and stripping down to his underwear, being shot more than twenty times while running, as directed, to a waiting police car. Eldridge Cleaver is also shot and beaten. Hutton dies. All surviving Panthers present are arrested for attempted murder. Cleaver jailed on parole violation.

April New York City chapter of BPP opens on Fulton St. in Brooklyn.

May Seattle chapter opens Free Breakfast Program. Eventually four Free Breakfast Programs will serve over 300 children daily.

June 6 Eldridge Cleaver released on bond; vows not to return to jail.

July Des Moines, Iowa chapter opens. The local BPP, together with local welfare rights and church groups, sponsors a breakfast program, welfare rights advocacy and various youth activities. Seattle BPP office is raided. Group of BPP members visit United Nations, speak with representatives of Third World nations and liberation movements about the plight of Black people and other people of color in the United States.

July 15 Huey Newton's trial begins at Alameda County

Courthouse. Massive "Free Huey" rally (over 5,000 people) receives worldwide attention.

August Indianapolis, Indiana chapter opens. Newark, NJ, BPP office firebombed. Bobby Seale speaks in Chicago during the Democratic Party National Convention, at the massive counterdemonstration called by the Students for a Democratic Society (S.D.S.), which ended in police rampage, beatings and arrests.

August 25 BPP members Steve Bartholomew, Robert Lawrence and Tommy Lewis are murdered by Los Angeles police as they stop to buy gas.

September 7 Southern California Chicano group "Brown Berets" attend funeral of the three BPP/LA members shot on August 25.

September 8 In a compromise verdict, jury convicts Huey Newton of manslaughter and aquits him of assault charge. FBI Director J. Edgar Hoover calls the BPP "the greatest threat to the internal security of the country."

September 28 Huey Newton is sentenced to 2-15 years in prison. Two on-duty Oakland police, admittedly drunk, shoot up the BPP headquarters and neighboring apartments. Then Police Chief Darryl Gates (later Chief of the Los Angeles P.D.) refuses to charge the officers with any offense, saying they were "a little tense and were blowing off steam."

September Eldridge Cleaver's parole is again overturned. Cleaver goes into hiding, later is granted political asylum in Cuba.

October BPP/NYC leaders Jordan Ford and David Brothers along with lawyers J. Leftcourt and William Kunstler, the Emergency Civil Liberties Committee, the Center for Constitutional Rights and the National Lawyers Guild file suit calling for decentralization of the N.Y.P.D. Police

1968 continued

attack BPP/NYC. Denver BPP office shot up in police attack.

October 15 BPP member Welton Armstead murdered in Seattle.

November 7 BPP member Sidney Miller killed in Seattle.

November 11 West Oakland BPP begins Free Breakfast Program.

November 25 FBI memo details plans to promote violence between the BPP and the Southern California-based organization, United Slaves (US). Its leader, Ron Karenga, was later exposed as cooperating with federal and local police agencies.

November Chicago chapter of BPP is officially recognized. Bobby Brown leads effort to form chapter.

December 7 Denver BPP office raided by police looking for "stolen military rifles." None were found, but police and firemen ignite the office with incendiaries, destroying thousands of dollars worth of food and toys that BPP members had been collecting to distribute during the upcoming holidays. Newark BPP office firebombed.

December 18 Indianapolis BPP office raided by FBI and local police.

December 21 BPP/Brooklyn participate in mass student demonstration for community control of schools.

December 27 Police raid Des Moines, Iowa, BPP office.

December 30 Franko Diggs, a member of the BPP/Los Angeles chapter, is shot in the back of the head by police agents.

December Bobby Seale attends World Peace Conference in Montreal, Canada; expresses full support of the BPP for the National Liberation Front of South Vietnam.

December BPP/Chicago, joined by Fred Hampton and Brad Greene, works to forge peace and unity between Black, Puerto Rican and white street gangs as well as the S.D.S.

1969

January Kansas City, Missouri chapter opens, works closely with local Methodist Inner City Parish on free breakfast program, welfare rights, a community drug program, trash clean-up and other service projects. BPP/KC makes agreement with police that recognized community leaders would accompany police on any searches of BPP offices or residences. K.C. Police Dept. subsequently violates this agreement.

January 17 BPP/Southern California leaders Alprentice "Bunchy" Carter, and John Jerome Huggins are murdered on UCLA campus by members of the US (United Slaves) organization. Almost simultaneously, the LAPD raids several BPP offices in Los Angeles area. Four months later (May 23), BPP member John Savage is killed by US members in San Diego, possibly to keep him from testifying at the trial for the above murders.

January 24 Chicago police and the FBI conspire to prevent BPP leader Fred Hampton from appearing on a TV talk show.

January 25 BPP national headquarters enacts a membership purge to "eliminate provocateurs and members whose conduct is detrimental to the welfare of the community and the Party."

January 30 FBI Director J. Edgar Hoover approves mailing of anonymous letter to provoke Blackstone Rangers to attack BPP in Chicago.

February BPP/Brooklyn members work with students at Canarsie High in demanding a holiday for Human Rights

1969 *continued*

leader Malcolm X and the establishment of a cultural center in the school.

March BPP/Chicago starts first of their three Free Breakfast programs, and assists a Black student group as well as a street gang (the Black Disciples) in developing their own breakfast programs.

March 20 Bobby Seale indicted for violating the federal anti-riot act in his speech at the 1968 Chicago Democratic Convention.

April BPP/LA office raided.

April 2 New York police serve warrants for arrest of twenty-one BPP/NY members on a wide assortment of "conspiracy" charges, from conspiracy to rob subway token booths to conspiracy to bomb department stores and a botanical garden. Those arrested are held on $100,000 bail.

April 26 Des Moines, Iowa, BPP offices destroyed in anonymous bombing. Police refuse to investigate.

April 28 San Francisco BPP office raided by new police SWAT teams.

May BPP/Harlem helps develop four Free Breakfast programs as well as political education and housing advocacy programs. FBI orders all bureaus to sabotage BPP Free Breakfast programs.

May 1 California State Supreme Court begins hearing appeal of Huey Newton's conviction. 10,000 people rally.

May 21 BPP member Alex Rackley murdered outside New Haven, Connecticut.

May 22 BPP/New Haven, Connecticut office raided and eight members, including Erika Huggins, arrested on variety of "conspiracy" and murder charges.

June Arkansas Senator John McClellan leads an Internal

Security Committee "witch hunt" against the BPP.

June 4 Detroit BPP office raided.

June 6 BPP Central Committee member Landon Williams and Rory Hithe arrested and charged with murder and conspiracy.

June 7 Chicago BPP office raided.

June 15 San Diego and Sacramento BPP offices raided.

Spring BPP conducts a purge to consolidate national organization and instill Party discipline. Many long-time members are expelled and entire chapters are closed. BPP membership is frozen and no new chapters are to open. Much of the original leadership is now in jail or in exile. BPP members and community in general are aware that police infiltration of BPP is at an all-time high. BPP members now required to give full-time commitment. They often live in communal arrangements. National Headquarters in Oakland sends BPP members Donald Cox, Al Carrol, Landon Williams and Rory Hithe to NY in order to help fill the leadership void created by the arrest of the NY Panther 21.

June 27 Winston-Salem, North Carolina group, National Committee to Combat Fascism (NCCF), begins work on the issue of Political Prisoners.

July Richmond, California BPP starts Liberation School. Brunch and snacks are provided during the day. Curriculum consists of Black History, writing skills and political science.

July 18–21 BPP sponsors a highly successful United Front Against Fascism Conference in Oakland, with NCCF. Progressive people from all backgrounds invited; organizations such as the Young Lords, Young Patriots, SDS, Republic of New Afrika, SNCC, and Red Guard participate.

July 24 Internal Revenue Service creates an Activists

1969 *continued*

Organization Project (later called Special Services Staff) and targets BPP.

July 31 Chicago BPP office raided.

August 15 BPP member Sylvester Bell murdered in San Diego by US organization members.

August 19 Bobby Seale arrested on charges of conspiracy to riot and to incite riot from 1968 Chicago Democratic Convention. Seale posts bail and is immediately re-arrested on murder and conspiracy charges from the Alex Rackley murder trial in New Haven, Connecticut (May 21).

August Katherine and Eldridge Cleaver are granted political asylum in Algeria.

Summer BPP proposes prisoner exchange between North Vietnam/Viet Cong and the United States government. The U.S. would release Huey Newton and other political prisoners and the Vietnamese would free captured U.S. soldiers. The National Liberation Front (NLF) agrees to the proposal in principle. BPP requests relatives of POW's to contact them. Parts of The Black Panther newspaper are printed in Spanish, mainly to assist a California Chicano organization La Raza in organizing.

Fall BPP forms National Committee to Combat Fascism offices; white people are invited to participate.

September 4 BPP member Larry Robertson dies of police-inflicted gunshot wounds.

September 8 Watts BPP Free Breakfast program raided by armed police.

September 12 BPP member Nathaniel Clark murdered in Los Angeles.

October 4 Chicago BPP office raided for the third time.

October 10 BPP members Bruce Richards and Walter Touré

Poke are stopped by members of the LAPD Metro Squad, who claim they were about to hold up a Jack-in-the-Box restaurant. In shoot-out, Poke is killed, Richards is wounded and charged with attempted murder.

November 13 BPP member Spurgeon "Jake" Winters, 19, murdered by Chicago police. Winters is said to have killed four policemen and wounded seven in the attack.

November 20 Albany, NY, BPP office attacked.

November 22 San Diego BPP office raided.

December 4 Illinois BPP leaders Fred Hampton and Mark Clark murdered in Chicago by police raiders from State Attorney's Office, in cooperation with FBI. Hampton, 21, was drugged beforehand by an agent provocateur who had infiltrated the BPP. Hampton was shot and killed in his sleep and Clark, 22, was killed as he answered a knock on the apartment door. Seven BPP members, several of whom were wounded, survived the attack.

December 8 BPP members in Central Avenue, LA headquarters, withstand a five-hour pre-dawn police attack. 18 BPP members arrested as LAPD simultaneously raids several offices.

December 15 ANC./South Africa, and ZAPU/ Zimbabwe, send letter of support to BPP.

December 17 The Black Panther managing editor, Big Man, is denied entrance to Denmark for speaking engagement.
December 25 BPP member Sterling Jones murdered in Chicago.

1970

January 3 Bobby Seale sends message to white progressive movement— defeat domestic imperialism— addressing whites' anti-war stance but lack of involvement in the struggle against racism at home.

1970 continued

January 4 Opening in Chicago of the Spurgeon "Jake" Winters People's Free Health Clinic, the first BPP preventive medical clinic.

January 9 BPP/Boston begins free clothing program.

January 17 BPP declares support for Eritrea Liberation struggle.

January 24 Milwaukee, Wis. BPP chapter disbanded due to a lack of discipline in leadership and lack of work in the Black community.

February 8 Mayor Uhlman of Seattle denies request from firearms division of U.S. Treasury Department for Seattle police to participate in a raid against BPP because, in his words, "it smacks of Gestapo-type tactics."

March 7 Chicago community holds "People's Inquest" into the killings of Fred Hampton and Mark Clark. BPP delegation attends Palestine support committee conference in Algeria.

March 21 San Francisco chapter establishes tenants' grievance committee. Boston and New York BPP chapters actively intercede on behalf of tenants in disputes with landlords.

April Central Committee member Louis (Randy) Williams and three others arrested, charged with assault on police.

April BPP gains international support: BPP Solidarity committees from France, Britain, Denmark, Belgium, the Netherlands, West Germany and Sweden hold conference in Frankfurt, declare support for BPP, offer assistance, and demand respective governments pressure U.S. to free its political prisoners.

April 12 Offices of the New York Law Commune and New York Panther 21 lawyers are set ablaze. Many files destroyed, some taken by law enforcement people.

April 25 Berkeley, California NCCF collects enough signatures to place the issue of community control of police on the ballot.

April 30 Baltimore BPP Free Breakfast program raided. Two weeks earlier the police commissioner stated he was starting a program of "harrassment" of the BPP, its programs and supporters.

May 1 Major BPP-sponsored rally on the New Haven Green to garner support for Panthers Lonnie McLucas, Bobby Seale and Ericka Huggins in their respective trials. Baltimore BPP office raided.

May 11 FBI memo to San Francisco office directs a "disruptive and disinformation" operation aimed at furnishing BPP National Headquarters with false and divisive information.

May 15 FBI orders all Bureau offices to disrupt distribution of *The Black Panther* newspaper.

May 29 California Court of Appeals reverses Huey Newton's manslaughter conviction but refuses to grant him bail pending the prosecution's appeal.

May 31 Shots are fired into Boston BPP free medical clinic.

June 13 BPP sends delegation to United Nations to gain support for domestic Third World people by Third World nations and liberation organizations.

July 17 Mt. Vernon, NY Black Community Information Center starts liberation school; lunch snacks served.

July 25 Omaha, Nebraska chapter of NCCF disbanded, months after the office/house was bombed.

July 27 BPP member Babatunde Omarwali murdered in Chicago.

July 28 Carl Hampton, founder/chairman of People's Party II in Houston, Texas, an organization modeled after the BPP, is murdered by police.

1970 continued

July 31 New Bedford, Massachusetts NCCF raided by over one hundred police looking for illegal weapons. On preceding day the NCCF held a press conference stating they would submit to a daytime search of the office/house. Indianapolis: a white motorcycle gang called the Grim Reapers begin shooting up Black community; Panthers are called for help. They set up an armed patrol in the community.

August 2 Hartford, Connecticut NCCF office/house raided by police who claim to be looking for a sniper on the roof.

August 5 Huey Newton is released after winning his appeal. He's spent three years in jail.

August 7 Jonathan Jackson (17 years old) raids Marin County Hall of Justice giving arms to prisoners James McClain, William Christmas, and Ruchell McGee. The four take hostage judge Harold Haley, the prosecutor and three jurors and leave in a van provided by police. Federal-directed police open fire on the van. In the ensuing shootout, William Christmas, James McClain, Jonathan Jackson and the judge were all killed by the police.

August 8 Michael "Cetewayo" Tabor of NY Panther 21 is released on bail after 16 months in jail. NCCF/Southern Illinois chapter founder Babatunde X Omarwali killed. BPP/Seattle starts program of busing visitors to state prisons.

August 11 BPP/LA Deputy Minister of Defense Geronimo Pratt fails to appear in court for LA 18 case.

August 15 BPP holds funeral for Jonathan Jackson; thousands attend. Newton reads eulogy, terming Jackson's and other's actions "revolutionary suicide."

August 21 NCCF/Winston-Salem starts free clothing program. Huey Newton calls for BPP and the entire movement to support women's liberation and gay rights.

August 29 Huey Newton officially offers Panther troops to the NLF of South Vietnam as a show of support for their struggle.

September 1 Philadelphia BPP offices raided. Police order BPP members to strip naked after being lined up in the street. Among those arrested is Mumia Abu-Jamal.

September 3 International section of BPP in Algeria officially opens. At ceremony Cleaver states BPP strategy as 1) Unite Black Americans; 2) Develop united front within United States; 3) Join international front against U.S. imperialism.

September 4–5 BPP convenes Plenary Session for Revolutionary Peoples Constitutional Convention in Philadelphia; over 10,000 people attend.

September 5 Newton holds press conference in Oakland, charges Stokely Carmichael with being a CIA agent.

October 2 Newton visits General Motors wildcat strike plant in Fremont, CA. BPP endorses strike, provides food for strikers' families.

October 6 NCCF/Washington Heights opens in Manhattan. BPP/NY works with Asian group I. Wor Kuen, Young Lords and other Puerto Rican groups as well as with grassroots housing organizations in setting up a housing crimes trial. It is held at Columbia University with BPP and other groups serving as judges.

October 15 NCCF/New Orleans office/house attacked by heavily-armed police and FBI agents, using an armored car/tank. BPP members battle police two and a half hours before surrendering. Police claim a police agent was discovered and beaten by Panthers. Panthers claim that they

1970 continued

put police informants out of the office and "the community dealt with them."

October 17 Young Lords member Julio Roden is killed in jail. BPP/Harlem participate in funeral. Newton holds press conference in support of Angela Davis.

October 31 BPP/Boston develops peer drug rehabilitation program called "Project Concern."

November 4 Police raid BPP/LA child care center. They hold guns on children while beating up an adult BPP member.

November 7 Southern California chapter Free Breakfast program serves over 1,700 meals per week; BPP/Boston program over 700 meals in a three-week period.

December FBI memo discusses plans for microphone and telephone surveillance of Huey Newton's Oakland apartment.

December 4-5 BPP convenes Revolutionary People's Constitutional Convention in Washington, D.C.

1971

January Oakland chapter opens a shoe manufacturing and repair program. Various S.F. Bay Area BPP chapters start day care centers. NCCF/Dayton, Ohio opens a Black Community information center, also holds political education classes and breakfast program.

January 16 NCCF/Toledo, Ohio establishes a legal assistance program with 24-hour hotline and free lawyer services. BPP/Chicago medical cadre goes door-to-door doing checkups and providing preventive health care information.

January 22 BPP/New Haven opens free health clinic.

January 23 Huey Newton purges BPP/S.Cal. Deputy

Minister of Defense Geronimo Pratt, along with Wilfred Cruch Holiday and George Lloyd, from BPP. "Any party members or community worker who attempts to aid them or communicate with them in any form or manner shall help to undermine and destroy the Black Panther Party," Newton states in an article.

Many members, both leadership and rank-and-file, are confused by these expulsions. In the NYC/Harlem branch, Pratt's political writings on guerrilla warfare were widely studied and many knew his reputation for Party discipline and strong revolutionary principles.

[This dissension was a direct result of the FBI's Counterintelligence Program. Years later, shortly before his own death, Huey Newton would apologize to Pratt for this mistake and offer to commit himself to getting Pratt out of prison, where Pratt remains today.]

January Huey Newton visits BPP houses/offices in New York, discovers there is a 60% decrease in the weapons; national leadership suspicious.

February BPP member Fred Bennett murdered in Santa Cruz mountains, a victim of COINTELPRO-inspired internecine strife.

February 13 "Enemies of the People" on front cover of *The Black Panther,* featuring pictures of Richard Dhoruba Moore and Michael Cetewayo Tabor, both BPP/NY leaders and Panther 21 defendants, as well as Connie Mathews, Newton's Secretary and former coordinator of BPP European Solidarity Committee. The three newly expelled members are thought to have left the country.

February Eldridge Cleaver issues a statement calling for the expulsion of Chief of Staff David Hilliard and for Huey Newton to stand trial to determine his revolutionary dedication. A group of East Coast BPP members holds a press

1971 continued

conference at the BPP/Harlem branch calling for the expulsion of David Hilliard and Huey Newton. They recognize Chairman Bobby Seale (still in prison), Minister of Information Eldridge Cleaver, Communications Secretary Kathleen Cleaver and Field Marshall Donald Cox as the Central Committee of the BPP. This marks the "split" amongst many chapters and members. NY chapter becomes national headquarters for new Panther faction.

March On a local San Francisco TV program direct phone hook-up with Algeria, Newton expels Cleaver and the entire International Section. Cleaver calls Huey Newton a "madman."

March 5 BPP sponsors "Intercommunal Day of Solidarity dedicated to Freedom for all Political Prisoners."

March 8 Robert Webb slain in NYC by members of the "Oakland faction" of COINTELPRO-engineered split.

March *Right On* newspaper is put out by East Coast BPP.

April FBI claims to have ended this month its infamous COINTELPRO operations which have by now successfully created an open split and initiated fratricide within the BPP.

April FBI begins payment of rent on apartment across the hall from Huey P. Newton.

April BPP activists forced "underground." Black Liberation Army (BLA) initiates armed community retaliation against racist police attacks.

April 10 BPP initiates nationwide campaign to research and eradicate Sickle Cell Anemia, deadly hereditary blood disease primarily affecting Black people.

April 17 BPP member Samuel Napier, circulation manager of The Black Panther (now the paper of the West Coast faction) is tortured and killed in New York. The distribution office is burned to the ground. Oakland faction blames NY faction. BPP/BLA member Harold Russell shot and killed by NYPD as he lay wounded in a Harlem basement.

Spring BPP members across the nation begin taking sides between the two factions. Donald Cox, Eldridge and Kathleen Cleaver of the Central Committee side with the East Coast. Newton, Hilliard, Bobby and John Seale as well as Douglas and George Jackson side with the West Coast, which, being the original base of the BPP, attracted far more chapters. Many expelled and self-removed members of the BPP such as the Panther 21 defendants and Geronimo Pratt are readily welcomed by the East Coast faction. They soon assume leadership positions. Many who were expelled and/or arrested for conducting armed acts were supported by the East Coast faction.

May New York Panther 21 trial ends after 26 months in acquittal on all counts. Panthers Michael Cetewayo Tabor, Richard Dhoruba Moore and Edward Jamal Joseph acquitted in absentia.

May 24 Ericka Huggins and Bobby Seale to be released from over two years' incarceration. The judge declares a mistrial, granting defense motions to dismiss the charges.

June 28 Second trial of Huey Newton begins at Alameda County Courthouse.

July BPP boycott two liquor stores in California which refuse to contribute to BPP Survival Programs.

July 23 Three days after opening of LA 18 trial, former BPP member Melvin Cotton Smith reveals himself to be a long-time undercover agent provocateur and testifies for the prosecution.

August 8 Second trial of Huey Newton ends in a hung jury.

1971 continued

August 18 Cleveland BPP Free Health Clinic dynamited.

August 21 BPP Field Marshall George Jackson assassinated at San Quentin Prison; three guards and two "turncoats" killed.

From the FBI Panther Files
Counterintelligence Program (COINTELPRO) Targeting of the Black Panther Party

1. Letter from J. Edgar Hoover to Special Agent in Charge, Albany, New York

3/4/68

To: SAC, Albany   PERSONAL ATTENTION
From: Director, FBI   (100-448006)
COUNTERINTELLIGENCE PROGRAM
BLACK NATIONALIST–HATE GROUPS
RACIAL INTELLIGENCE

Title is changed to substitute Racial Intelligence for Internal Security for Bureau routing purposes.

BACKGROUND

By letter dated 8/25/67 the following offices were advised of the beginning of a Counterintelligence Program against militant Black Nationalist Hate Groups:

Albany	Memphis
Atlanta	Newark
Baltimore	New Orleans

Boston	New York
Buffalo	Philadelphia
Charlotte	Phoenix
Chicago	Pittsburgh
Cincinnati	Richmond
Cleveland	St. Louis
Detroit	San Francisco
Jackson	Washington
Los Angeles	

Each of the above offices was to designate a Special Agent to coordinate this program. Replies to this letter indicated an interest in counterintelligence against militant Black nationalist groups that foment violence and several offices outlined procedures which had been effective in the past. For example, Washington Field Office had furnished information about a new Nation of Islam (NOI) grade school to appropriate authorities in the District of Columbia who investigated to determine if the school conformed to the District regulations for private schools. In the process WFO obtained background information on the parents of each pupil.

The Revolutionary Action Movement (RAM), a pro-Chinese communist group, was active in Philadelphia, Pa., in the summer of 1967. The Philadelphia Office alerted local police, who then put RAM leaders under close scrutiny. They were arrested on every possible charge until they could no longer make bail. As a result, RAM leaders spent most of the summer in jail and no violence traceable to RAM took place.

The Counterintelligence Program is now being expanded to include 41 offices. Each of the offices added to this program should designate an Agent familiar with black nationalist activity and interested in counterintelligence, to coordinate this program. This Agent will be responsible for the periodic progress letters being requested, but each Agent working this type of case should participate in the formulation of counterintelligence operations.

GOALS

For maximum effectiveness of the Counterintelligence Program, and to prevent wasted effort, long-range goals are being set.

1. Prevent the <u>coalition</u> of militant black nationalist groups. In unity there is strength; a truism that is no less valid for all its triteness. An effective coalition of black nationalist groups might be the first step toward a real "Mau Mau" in America, the beginning of a true revolution.

2. Prevent the <u>rise of a "messiah"</u> who could unify, and electrify, the militant black nationalist movement. Malcolm X might have been such a "messiah;" he is the martyr of the movement today. Martin Luther King, Stokely Carmichael, and Elijah Muhammed all aspire to this position. Elijah Muhammed is less of a threat because of his age. King could be a very real contender for this position should he abandon his supposed "obedience" to "white, liberal doctrines" (nonviolence) and embrace black nationalism. Carmichael has the necessary charisma to be a real threat in this way.

3. Prevent <u>violence</u> on the part of black nationalist groups. This is of primary importance, and is of course, a goal of our investigative activity; it should also be a goal of the Counterintelligence Program. Through counterintelligence it should be possible to pinpoint potential troublemakers and neutralize them before they exercise their potential for violence.

4. Prevent militant black nationalist groups and leaders from gaining <u>respectability</u>, by discrediting them to three separate segments of the community. The goal of discrediting black nationalists must be handled tactically in three ways. You must discredit these groups and individuals to, first, the responsible Negro community. Second, they must be discredited to the white community, both the responsible community and to "liberals" who have vestiges of sympathy for militant black nationalists simply because they are Negroes. Third, these groups must be discredited in the eyes of

Negro radicals, the followers of the movement. This last area requires entirely different tactics from the first two. Publicity about violent tendencies and radical statements merely enhances black nationalists to the last group; it adds "respectability" in a different way.

5. A final goal should be to prevent the long-range <u>growth</u> of militant black nationalist organizations, especially among youth. Specific tactics to prevent these groups from converting young people must be developed.

Besides these five goals counterintelligence is a valuable part of our regular investigative programs as it often produces positive information.

TARGETS

Primary targets of the Counterintelligence Program, Black Nationalist-Hate Groups, should be the most violent and radical groups and their leaders. We should emphasize these leaders and organaizations that are nationwide in scope and are most capable of disrupting this country. These targets should include the radical and violence-prone leaders, members, and followers of the:

> Student Nonviolent Coordinating Committee (SNCC)
> Southern Christian Leadership Conference (SCLC)
> Revolutionary Action Movement (RAM)
> Nation of Islam (NOI)

Offices handling these cases and those of Stokely Carmichael of SNCC, H. Rap. Brown of SNCC, Martin Luther King of SCLC, Maxwell Stanford of RAM, and Elijah Muhammed of NOI, should be alert for counterintelligence suggestions.

INSTRUCTIONS

Within 30 days of the date of this letter each office should:

1. Advise the Bureau of the identity of the Special Agent assigned to coordinate this program.

2. Submit a very succinct summary of the black nationalist movement in the field office territory. Include name, number of

members and degree of activity of each black nationalist group. Also state your estimate of each group's propensity for violence. This is for target evaluation only, not for record militant black nationalists and any other militant black nationalist leaders who might be future targets of counterintelligence action because of their propensity for violence. Include a minimum of background information on each person listed; a few descriptive sentences should suffice.

3. List those organizations and individuals you consider of such potential danger as to be considered for current counterintelligence action. Briefly justify each target.

4. Submit any suggestion you have for overall counterintelligence action of the administration of this program. Suggestions for action against any specific target should be submitted by separate letter.

5. Submit, by separate letter, suggestions for counterintelligence action against the targets previously listed as field-wide. These should not be general, such as "publicize Stokely Carmichael's travel to communist countries," but should be specific as to target, what is to be done, what contacts are to be used, and all other information needed for the Bureau to approve a counterintelligence operation.

Thereafter, on a ninety-day basis, each office is to submit a progress letter summarising counterintelligence operations proposed during the period, operations effected, and tangible results. Any changes in the overall black nationalist movement should be summarized in this letter. This should include new organaizations, new leaders, and any changes in data listed under number two above. Suggestions for counterintelligence operations should not be set out in this progess letter. Use the following captions.

1. Operations Under Consideration, 2. Operations being Effected, 3. Tangible Results, and 4. Developments of Counterintelligence Interest.

These 90-day progress letters are due at the Bureau the first day of March, June, September, and December, excepting March, 1968.

The effectiveness of counterintelligence depends on the quality and quantity of positive information available regarding the target and on the imagination and initiative of Agents working the program. The response of the field to the Counterintelligence Program against the Communist Party, USA, indicates that a superb job can be done by the field on counterintelligence.

Counterintelligence operations must be approved by the Bureau. Because of the nature of this program each operation must be designed to protect the Bureau's interest so that there is no possibility of embarrassment to the Bureau. Beyond this the Bureau will give every possible consideration to your proposals.

NOTE:

See memorandum G.C. Moore to Mr. W.C. Sullivan captioned as above dated 2/29/68, prepared by TJD:rmn.

2. Letter from Supervisor John J. Kearney

SUPERVISOR JOHN J. KEARNEY:
The Black Panther Party JJK:egb 4/16/69

(BPP) as constituted in the New York City (NYC) area is a most elusive organization. Leadership is constantly changing, organizational structure regularly broken, and membership fluctuating with a rapid turnover. At any given time over the past six months hardcore membership (those BPP members who work on projects and/or assignments) generally number about fifty.

The New York Office (NYO) has had an extremely aggressive program designed to develop informants within the BPP as well as deter individuals from joining and/or remaining within the BPP. To date we have conducted approximately five hundred interviews. Condiderable success has been obtained from this investigative approach. Included in this program has been the interview of the parents of children who were associated with the BPP. The overall effect of this program is perhaps best expressed by a ▬▬▬▬▬ who came to New York City and was informed by BPP leadership that the Federal Bureau of Investigation (FBI) has been talking to the parents of BPP members. These parents have panicked when they heard their children were in the BPP and have made them drop out.

In addition to the interview program we have had a program of arresting BPP members. To date eleven BPP members have been arrested as a result of this program. Arrests arose out of firebombings, possession of dynamite, and crime aboard an aircraft.

According to Bureau of Special Services, New York City Police Department (BSS, NYCPD), Kings County Special Unit, NYCPD and other sources these programs have severely hampered and disrupted the BPP, particularly in Brooklyn, New York, where for a while BPP operations were at a complete standstill and in fact have never recovered sufficiently to operate effectively.

this year BPP activity in the NYC area was at a minimum. He stated that what energy there was had been rapidly dissipated by the BPP striving to make bail money available for those arrested, hence it was impossible to have a BPP program.

there is no adequate leadership in the New York BPP. It lacks an effective organizer and initiative. There has been a basic failure to accomplish anything of substance in the New York area.

3. Letter from Special Agent in Charge, New York City to FBI Director J. Edgar Hoover

TO: DIRECTOR, FBI (100-448006)11/3/69
FROM: SAC, NEW YORK (100-161140)

> ALL INFORMATION CONTAINED
> HEREIN IS UNCLASSIFIED
> DATE 7-22-70 BY SP3

COUNTER INTELLIGENCE PROGRAM
BLACK NATIONALIST-HATE GROUPS
RACIAL INTELLIGENCE-BPP

The following successful counterintelligence action taken by the NYO with respect to the Black Panther Party (BPP) Breakfast Program is set forth for information purposes.

On 10/28/69, information was received that CHARLENE LANE, BPP Free Breakfast Program Coordinator had contacted a priest at St. Anthony's Church, somewhere in New York, and made arrangements to institute a Breakfast Program at the church.

Investigation by the NYO determined that the church referred to was probably St. Anthony of Padua, 832 East 166th St., Bronx, NY, and the priest possibly one Father STELTZ.

On 10/29/69, Father STELTZ was interviewed by SAS JOHN T. DOWNEY and JAMES G. FITZGERALD. He stated that he had been approached by one CHARLENE LANE from the BPP on 10/27/69. She requested space at St. Anthony's in order that the BPP could serve free breakfast to the local children. She said the food would be solicited from local merchants, the BPP would serve it and the BPP would clean the premises after breakfast.

Father STELTZ stated that he readily agreed to the program but stipulated to CHARLENE LANE that no political overtures could be made to the children. She agreed and he approved of the program which was to begin on 11/3/69. Father STELTZ stated that he was aware of the reputation of the BPP, but felt that he could oversee the program and control it fully.

The interviewing agents proceeded to fully discuss the BPP with Father STELTZ. It was pointed out to him that while, as he stated, he is aware of the BPP reputation, such action on his part would provide the BPP with an aura of respectability. The agents related to him the problems which could arise should he one day decide to discontinue the program after it started. Children would have been indoctrinated with BPP ideology, others in his school would be recruited into the BPP, parents would be discontented with a discontinuation of free breakfast and local merchants would be chagrined at possibly being forcibly persuaded to give free food to Father STELTZ.

Father STELTZ appeared apprehensive at the possible repercussions of such a program and stated that he knew of no way to call it off at this late date.

He was advised that another Pastor, in a similar situation, called a meeting of his Parish Council (PC) submitted the BPP program to them and by unanimous vote the PC voted against the idea.

Father STELTZ thanked the agents for their consideration of his problem and expressed his appreciation for the FBI alerting him to what could have been a disastrous situation. In conclusion, he stated that he would call an emergency meeting of his non-existent Parish Council and advise the BPP of the decision not to have a BPP sponsored Free Breakfast Program.

On 11/3/69, Father STELTZ was recontacted at which time he stated that the BPP Free Breakfast Program did not begin as planned on this date nor would he permit it at St. Anthony's in the future.

4. FBI Telegram from Director
to Los Angeles and New York Offices

8PM URGENT 6-9-70 JTJ
LOS ANGELES (157-1503)
NEW YORK (100-161993)
DIRECTOR (100-161993) IP

BLACK PANTHER PARTY (BPP) — FACTIONALISM, RACIAL MATTERS.

RENYTEL JUNE FIVE LAST.

LA AUTHORIZED TO SEND TELEGRAM TO CURTIS POWELL, NYC, AS REQUESTED BY NY. INSURE TELEGRAM SENT IN MANNER THAT CANNOT BE TRACED TO BUREAU. ADVISE BUREAU AND PERTINENT OFFICES WHEN SENT. NY SUBMIT DETAILS OF FACTIONALISM IN LHM FOR DISSEMINATION.

ALL RECIPIENTS SUBMIT BY AIRTEL ADDITIONAL COUNTERINTELLIGENCE PROPOSALS UNDER COUNTERINTELLIGENCE CAPTION TO FURTHER EXPLOIT THIS FACTIONALISM ON CONTINUING BASIS. AIRMAIL COPIES TO SF AND WH.

NEW YORK

5. Telegram from Director's Office to New York Office

10:40AM URGENT 6-18-70 LRC
TO   NEW YORK (100-161140)
FROM   DIRECTOR (100-448006) 2P

COUNTERINTELLIGENCE PROGRAM, BLACK NATIONAL-
IST-HATE GROUPS, RACIAL INTELLIGENCE, BLACK PAN-
THER PARTY (BPP)

RENYTEL JUNE SIXTEEN LAST.
NEW YORK IS AUTHORIZED TO DISCREETLY FURNISH
DATA AS OUTLINED IN RETEL TO ████████████████████

IN AN EFFORT TO OBTAIN NEWS MEDIA PUBLICITY
HIGHLIGHTING FRICTION BETWEEN EAST AND WEST
COAST BPP LEADERSHIP PERSONNEL.
INSURE THIS ACTIVITY IS HANDLED IN MANNER TO
PRECLUDE ITS BEING TRACED TO THE BUREAU. PROMPT-
LY ADVISE OF SUBSEQUENT COUNTERINTELLIGENCE
BENEFITS DERIVED UNDER INSTANT CAPTION.
NEW YORK AUTHORIZED CONDUCT INTERVIEW BPP
MEMBER RICHARD MOORE AFTER CLEARING SAME
THROUGH LOCAL AUTHORITIES IN VIEW PENDING CRIMI-
NAL CHARGES HIS REGARD. RESULTS OF INTERVIEW OF
MOORE SHOULD BE FURNISHED BUREAU UNDER HIS CAP-
TION IN FORM SUITABLE FOR DISSEMINATION TOGETHER
WITH RECOMMENDATIONS FOR ADDITIONAL INVESTIGA-
TIVE ACTION IN HIS REGARD. HANDLE PROMPTLY.
END
PAC   FBI NEW YORK

6. Telegram from Special Agent in Charge, New Haven, Connecticut, to Director, FBI

DATE: 6/5/70

AIRTEL

TO: DIRECTOR, FBI   (100-448006)
FROM: SAC, NEW HAVEN   (157-785)
SUBJECT: COUNTERINTELLIGENCE PROGRAM
  BLACK NATIONALIST HATE GROUPS
  RACIAL INTELLIGENCE- BLACK PANTHER PARTY (BPP)

ReBuairtel to Charlotte 5/27/70 and NY airtel 6/4/70.

New Haven concurs with NYO re the letter to be directed to BPP headquarters, NYC, concerning DOUGLAS MIRANDA and would, of course, alter the format and not the content of letter suggested by NYO.

NHO suggests the following letter to BPP, New Haven, regarding the internal struggle involving MIRANDA, ROBERT BAY and DHARUBA (RICHARD MOORE, of the Panther Twenty One.)

"Panther Pad, Conn.

"You hafta know I saw Doug around the courthouse Tuesday. Man he don't like bein down south. He says he thinks Bay is play ball with the pigs—also he says Dharuba don't want any part of Bay. If Bay is gettin piggy we have a big problem.

Power to the People"

New Haven airtel 6/2/70 advised Bureau of MIRANDA's presence at Superior Court, New Haven, that date (or last Tuesday). The Bureau has been apprised of the simmering rift between BAY and DHARUBA.

7. Telegram from New York Office to Director, FBI

RENYTEL JUNE SIXTEEN LAST.

7/20/70

AIRTEL

TO: DIRECTOR, FBI (157-12340)
FROM: SAC, NEW YORK (157-3357)
SUBJECT: RICHARD MOORE

                    RM—BPP

ReButel to NY dated 6/18/70, captioned "COUNTERINTELLI-GENCE PROGRAM, BLACK NATIONALIST-HATE GROUPS, RACIAL INTELLIGENCE, BLACK PANTHER PARTY (BPP)".

NYC authorities have been contacted and advised that they had no objection to agents of the FBI interviewing subject.

On 6/17/70, ▮▮▮▮▮▮▮▮ advised that subject has been trans-ferred to the Brooklyn Branch of the BPP, 180 Sutter Ave., Brooklyn, NY, NY, and will function out of that office. No current address could be learned for subject.

Close contact has been maintained with ▮▮▮▮▮▮▮ in an effort to learn subject's movements and residence, with negative results.

On 6/28/70, 7/10/70, 7/15/70 - 7/17/70, surveillances were con-ducted in the vicinity of the BPP, 180 Sutter St., Brooklyn, NY, in an effort to locate and eventually isolate subject for interview. The results of these surveillance were negative.

On 7/16/70, ▮▮▮▮▮▮▮ 162 West 141st ST., NYC, subject's former address, advised that he put subject and his wife out of the apartment approximately three months ago when he learned that sub-ject was a member of the BPP. ▮▮▮▮▮▮▮▮▮ stated he has not seen subject nor does he have a forwarding address for him.

8. Telegram from Director, FBI
to Special Agent in Charge, New York

8/24/70

TO: SAC, New York   (100-161140)
FROM: Director, FBI   (100-448006)

COUNTERINTELLIGENCE PROGRAM
BLACK NATIONALIST- HATE GROUPS
RACIAL INTELLIGENCE
(BLACK PANTHER PARTY)

Reurairtel 8-11-70

You are authorized to prepare and mail anonymous letters No. 1 and No. 2 set forth in re airtel and anonymous letter No. 3 as revised by the Bureau and set forth below. Take usual precautions to insure letters cannot be traced to Bureau. Advise Bureau and interested offices of positive results achieved.

Your proposed anonymous letter No. 3 has been revised slightly by the Bureau to strengthen its authenticity and is set forth below:

"Brothers,

"I am employed by the State of California and have been close to Huey Newton while he was in jail.

"Let me warn you that this pretty nigger may very well be working for pig Reagon. I don't know why he was set free but I am suspicious. I got this ideaa because he had privileges in jail like the trustees get. He had a lot of privacy most prisoners don't get. I don't think all his private meetings were for sex. I am suspicious of him.

"Don't tell Newton too much if he starts asking you questions—it may go right back to the pigs.

Power to the People"

9. Telegram from Director, FBI to Special Agents in Charge, New York and San Francisco

Airtel   2/3/71
To: SACs, New York (100-161993)
            San Francisco (157-601)
From: Director, FBI (100-448006)

COINTELPRO—BLACK PANTHER PARTY (BPP)
EXPULSIONS — RACIAL MATTERS

ReNYtel to Bureau and San Francisco 2/1/71.

Bureau concurs generally with New York's proposed letter from "New York 21" to Eldridge Cleaver in Algeria. However, two changes are desired.

Paragraph five should be changed to read "As the leading theoretician of the party's philosophy and as brother among brothers, we urge you to make your influence felt. We think that The Rage is the only person strong enough to pull this factionalized party back together."

Also the word "expulsion" should be deleted from the last paragraph.

Bureau feels above changes necessary since purpose of letter is not to cause Cleaver to plead or reason with Newton but rather to cause as much dissension as possible within BPP, particularly between Newton and Cleaver.

New York is authorized to send the letter proposed in referenced teletype to Cleaver with the above changes. Bureau agrees that the letter should be sent 24 to 48 hours after "The Black Panther" newspaper reporting the expulsion of the "New York 21" reaches the streets. If such an article does not appear in "The Black Panther,"

mailing of the letter should be held in abeyance and additional recommendations made in that regard.

New York should insure that this mailing connot be traced to
the Bureau, and New York and San Francisco advise the Bureau of
any results of the counterintelligence activity.

10. Informative Note

Domestic Intelligence Division

INFORMATIVE NOTE

Date 2-9-71

Attached is a proposed counterintelligence letter by our San
Francisco Office in order to further promote dissension and distrust
in the Black Panther Party (BPP). Fred B. in attached alludes to Fred
Bennett reportedly recently killed by BPP associates.

As a result of our counterintelligence program a considerable
amount of dissension and distrust has been created within the BPP
which has resulted in confusion among its members, suspension and
expulsion of others. If you approve, San Francisco Office will be
instructed to prepare and send letter mentioned in attached in a manner which cannot be traced back to the Bureau.

11. Telegram from San Francisco Office to Director, FBI

2:45PM URGENT   2/9/71   MCC
TO: DIRECTOR (100-448006)
FROM: SAN FRANCISCO (157-601) 2P
COINTELPRO — BLACK EXTREMISTS, RACIAL MATTERS.

TO PROMOTE DISSENSION AND DISTRUST BETWEEN HUEY NEWTON AND ELDRIDGE CLEAVER, BUREAU PERMISSION IS REQUESTED TO FORWARD FOLLOWING COMMUNICATION SPECIAL DELIVERY FROM SANTACRUZ, CALIFORNIA, TO ████████████ HUEY NEWTON, IN OAKLAND, CALIFORNIA. THE "AC" MIGHT BE CONSTRUED BY NEWTON TO BE ██████████ WHOSE WHEREABOUTS HAVE NOT BEEN KNOWN TO THE BPP FOR SEVERAL WEEKS.

"DEAR BROTHER—

"PLEASE WARN HUEY. HE DOESN'T KNOW THE DANGER HE IS IN. HUEY HAS HANDED OUT SUSPENSIONS AND DISCIPLINE WHOLESALE WITH NO IDEA OF WHO IS LOYAL AND WHO IS NOT.

"WHERE DOES HE THINK ALL OF OUR TROUBLE STARTED. WHY DOESN'T HE LOOK TO ALGIERS AND FIGURE IT OUT? FIRST HE LOST THE SUPPORT OF A GOOD PART OF THE WHITE RADICALS AND NOW THE NEW YORK CHAPTER.

WE STILL HAVE PEOPLE AT NATIONAL WHO ARE CLOSE TO NEW YORK AND ALGIERS. HUEY SHOULD BE CAREFUL BECAUSE WHEN ██████████ ARRIVES HE MAY END UP LIKE ████████████████████

"AC".
END
H
AJP FBI WASH DC

12. Telegram from San Francisco Office to New York, New Haven, and Director's Office

58 PM   NITEL 2-9-71   MRM
TO: DIRECTOR
       NEW YORK
       NEW HAVEN
FROM: SAN FRANCISCO (P) 2P
BLACK PANTHER PARTY—EXPULSIONS, RM—BPP.

A ███████████ THIS DATE ADVISED NEXT ISSUE OF BPP NEWSPAPER WILL CONTAIN ARTICLE ENTITLED "ENE-MIES OF THE PEOPLE", DENOUNCING AND EXPELLING CONNIE MATHEWS TABOR, MICHAEL TABOR AND RICHARD MOORE FOR THE FOLLOWING REASONS:

ONE: MOORE AT NEW HAVEN LAST WEEK BITTERLY CRITICIZED NEWTON AND IMPLIED HE INTENDED TO KILL HIM.

TWO: CONNIE MATHEWS TABOR HAD DISAPPEARED TWO FIVE, LAST, STEALING DETAILS OF HUEY NEWTON'S EASTERN SPEAKING TOUR AND THE EUROPEAN CON-TACTS NECESSARY FOR INTERCOMMUNAL SOLIDARITY DAY.

THREE: MICHAEL TABOR AND EDDIE JOSEPHS HAD DISAPPEARED WITH CONNIE.

FOUR: TABOR AND MOORE FAILED TO APPEAR FOR TRIAL IN NEW YORK FEBRUARY EIGHT LAST.

FIVE: CONNIE MATHEWS TABOR HAS CONTACTED A EUROPEAN PUBLISHER AND MADE PLANS TO PUBLISH A BOOK ABOUT THE BPP.

ARTICLE WILL POINT OUT THAT THE ABOVE ACTS

JEOPARDIZE THE LIVES OF BPP MEMBERS EVERYWHERE BY GIVING THE "PIGS" AN EXCUSE TO RAID BPP OFFICES (PRESUMBLY TO LOOK FOR MOORE AND TABOR).

ARTICLE WILL STATE THAT THE FACT THE NEW YORK TWENTY-ONE WERE EXPELLED BECAUSE OF THEIR LETTER TO THE WEATHERMEN CAN IN NO WAY JUSTIFY THE ACTIONS OF CONNIE MATHEWS TABOR, MICHAEL TABOR, AND RICHARD MOORE.

ADMINISTRATIVE:

ARTICLE WAS DICTATED FROM NEW YORK TO BPP HEADQUARTERS BY BETTY, PROBABLY, BETTY KENNER, WIFE OF MARTIN KENNER. SHE STATED ALL OF THE NEW YORK TWENTY-ONE WHO WERE IN JAIL WERE EXPELLED. THIS DID NOT INCLUDE AFENI SHAKUR AND JOAN BIRD.

BETTY ALSO STATED ROSAMARY MEALEY AND MARCIA ROBERTSON OF NEW HAVEN WERE ALSO EXPELLED.
END
RSP FBI WASH DC
JMC FBI NEW YORK

13. Letter from Special Agent
in Charge, New York Office to Director, FBI

3/2/71

FROM: SAC, NEW YORK (100-161140) (F)
TO: DIRECTOR, FBI (100-448006)
        COINTELPRO — BLACK EXTREMISTS

ReNYlet to the Bureau, dated 12/2/70.

1. <u>Operations Under Consideration</u>

The NYO is congnizant of the fact that the local operations of the BPP are in a chaotic state due to the unconsistent leadership techniques demonstrated by HUEY P. NEWTON and LEROY ELDRIDGE CLEAVER.

It is also apparent that one of the most active Black Extremist operations in the New York area is the distribution and sale of the BPP newspaper, "The Black Panther."

Both of the above-described situations have been selected as the main points to be exploited and attacked as part of the continuing counterintelligence program of the NYO.

2. <u>Operations Being Submitted</u>

On 12/3/70, the NYO proposed that a series of anti-BPP articles written by FRANZ TAGAE, a Ghanaian writer, be distributed to interested field offices as an aid in future counterintelligence efforts.

On 12/7/70, the NYO proposed that ▓▓▓▓▓▓▓▓▓ should be the target of future counterintelligence proposals by placing the blame on him for the failure of HUEY NEWTON to generate a good public image.

On 12/14/70, it was proposed that a letter from the Student Afro-American Society at Columbia University, New York City, should be directed to BPP National Headquarters, Oakland, California. This letter was critical of a speech delivered by HUEY NEWTON at New York City Community College.

On 12/14/70, it was proposed that a letter from a member of the Venceremos Brigade critical of the way Negroes are treated in Cuba should be sent to various SNCC members nationwide.

On 12/14/70, the NYO suggested that a letter aimed at disrupting any relatioinship which might exist between SNCC and the BPP should be mailed to various people in the New York City area.

On 12/21/70, it was proposed that a letter should be sent to HUEY NEWTON which was critical of the riotous living engaged in by certain BPP members in the New York area.

On 12/28/70, the Bureau granted authority for the Atlanta Office to implement a New York counterintelligence proposal set forth in New York letter to the Bureau dated 12/10/70.

On 1/20/71, the NYO proposed that a letter to the Editors of the local New York newspapers complaining of the BPP activities in New York should be prepared and sent to those concerned. This proposal was approved by Bureau airtel dated 1/28/71.

On 1/28/71, an anonymous letter critical of HUEY NEWTON's activities was proposed to be sent to ELDRIDGE CLEAVER. Approval for this letter was given by the Bureau on 2/3/71.

On 2/1/71, the NYO proposed that a letter critical of HUEY NEWTON's handling of the "Panther 21" matter should be sent to ELDRIDGE CLEAVER. This proposal did receive Bureau approval on 2/3/71.

On 2/4/71, the NYO suggested that a plethora of letters should be sent to HUEY NEWTON which would be critical of his recent receptions by college students during his speaking tours.

On 2/11/71, Bureau approval was granted to New York to act on its proposal of 2/10/71, to send a letter to ELDRIDGE CLEAVER, as well as distributing copies of a critical article on the BPP which appeared in the "New York Times."

On 2/11/71, it was proposed that a postcard should be sent to HUEY NEWTON complaining of the activities of particular members of the BPP.

On 2/16/71, a proposal to send a letter to HUEY NEWTON signed by a ficticious member of Youth Against War and Fascism was approved by Bureau airtel dated 2/22/71.

On 2/19/71, the NYO proposed that   should be the recipient of an anonymous counterintelligence letter.

3. Tangible Results

Since the submission of referenced letter, the BPP has undergone a complete bouleversement in its organization and operations in the New York City area. New York feels that the unsuccessful attempt by the BPP to hold the Revolutionary Peoples' Constitutional Convention in Washington, D.C., in the later part of 1970, as well as the abject failure of HUEY P. NEWTON in his attempt to attract a following by speaking at various East Coast colleges and universities, indicates some tangible results of captioned program.

It should also be noted that the split which has developed in the high level leadership of the BPP to wit the fallling out of NEWTON with CLEAVER, together with the purging of the "Panther 21" from the BPP, may be utilized as evidence that the couterintelligence efforts of the NYO have born [sic] some fruit.

4. Developments of Counteintelligence Interests

The aforementioned falling out of the various BPP leaders plus the disgruntled and undisciplined conduct of the rank and file BPP members presents future sources of counteintelligence objects and targets. This, along with the possibility of the New York area BPP members splitting entirely from the National BPP leadership, are points which the NYO feel can be capitalized on under this program.

The NYO will immediately inform the Bureau of any situations or developments that occur where counterintelligence techniques may be used.

No action will be taken on any counterintelligence proposals without prior bureau approval.

14. Letter from Special Agent in Charge, New York to Director, FBI

TO: DIRECTOR, FBI   (100-448006)   4/5/71
FROM: SAC, NEW YORK   (100-161140) (P)
          COINTELPRO — BLACK EXTREMISTS   RM
          ReNYlet to the Bureau, 3/2/71

Referenced letter pointed out that the Black Panther Party (BPP) had undergone a complete bouleversement in its organization and operations in the New York City area which left its local operations in a state of chaos.

Since the date of referenced letter, the BPP has split into two factions in the New York City area, namely the CLEAVER and NEWTON supporters. This dichotomy apparently has been instrumental in the shooting and killing of ROBERT WEBB, a functionary in the Cleaver faction in New York City.

These tumultuous events have made it difficult for the NYO to formulate specific and practical counterintelligence proposals which would be timely and productive.

New York feels that while at this time there are no specific proposals to be submitted, it is obvious that it would be deterimental to the continuing efforts of the BPP as a whole to keep the two opposed factions from reaching a detente or at least a rapprochement in their future dealings.

Inasmuch as the leadership of the Cleaver faction is without the continental boundaries of the United States, it will make it more difficult for that group to communicate with and control the operations of the rank and file membership of that group.

Therefore, this will make that faction more susceptible to counterintelligence techniques than the Newton faction.

New York will in the immediate future submit counterintelligence proposals against the Cleaver faction of the BPP designed to widen the existing rift within the BPP.

JLL: ss

15. Telegram from Director, FBI
to New York Office

NR 025 WA CODE
3:21PM NITEL   5-25-71 RSP
TO: NEW YORK (100-161569)
FROM: DIRECTOR (157-8415 SUB 34) 3P
BLACK NATIONALIST MOVEMENT - NEW YORK DIVISION,
RACIAL MATTERS

RENYTELS MAY TWENTY-TWO, LAST, CAPTIONED "TWO MEMBERS OF NEW YORK CITY POLICE DEPARTMENT (NYCPD) SHOT AND KILLED BY TWO NEGRO MALES, NYC, MAY TWENTY-ONE, ONE NINE SEVEN ONE, RACIAL MATTERS."

SHOOTING OF POLICE OFFICERS REFERRED TO IN RETELS IS THE SECOND SUCH INCIDENT OCCURRING IN NYC IN A FOUR-DAY PERIOD. ALL INDICATORS POINT TO INVOLVEMENT IN EACH INCIDENT BY BLACK EXTREMISTS WHO COULD WELL BELONG TO AN ORGANIZATION KNOWN AS THE "BLACK REVOLUTIONARY ARMY" CONCERNING WHICH YOUR OFFICE HAS INDICATED NO KNOWLEDGE.

TARGET AND DIRECT YOUR SOURCES AND INFORMANTS TO DETERMINE ALL FACTS INVOLVED AND THE POSSIBILITY THESE KILLINGS MAY BE LINKED TO THE WOUNDING OF TWO NYC POLICE OFFICERS ON MAY NINETEEN, LAST, AS PREVIOUSLY REPORTED BY YOUR OFFICE. CONDUCT INVESTIGATION BASED ON DATA RECEIVED FROM INFORMANTS. MAINTAIN CLOSE LIAISON WTH THE NYCPD TO DETERMINE COMPLETE INTELLIGENCE DATA AND TO IDENTIFY BLACK EXTREMIST INFLUENCE OR PARTICIPATION. INSURE YOUR INVESTI-

GATION DOES NOT INTERFERE WITH THE NYCPD'S MURDER INVESTIGATION AND THAT ANY PERTINENT DATA DEVELOPED REGARDING THE KILLER'S INDENTITIES AS RESULT OF OUR INTELLIGENCE INVESTIGATION IS IMMEDIATELY FURNISHED THAT AGENCY.

REVIEW APPROPRIATE FILES OF BLACK EXTREMIST ORGANIZATIONS, INCLUDING THOSE OF SO-CALLED THIRD WORLD GROUPS, IN ATTEMPT TO DEVELOP LOGICAL SUSPECTS. INCLUDE SUCH ORGANIZATIONS AND THEIR LEADERS IN TARGET ASSIGNMENTS GIVEN TO SOURCES. CONSIDER POSSIBILITY BOTH ATTACKS MAY BE RESULT OF REVENGE TAKEN AGAINST NYC POLICE BY THE BLACK PANTHER PARTY (BPP) AS A RESULT OF ITS ARREST OF BPP MEMBERS IN APRIL, ONE NINE SIX NINE, ON CHARGES OF CONSPIRACY TO COMMIT ARSON AND MURDER AND THE RELEASE OF EIGHT DEFENDANTS IN THAT CASE ON MAY THIRTEEN, ONE NINE SEVEN ONE. REGARDLESS OF WHETHER THE BPP MAY OR MAY NOT BE INVOLVED. THESE SHOOTINGS MAY TRIGGER OTHER ACTS OF VIOLENCE BY BLACK EXTREMISTS IN THE NYC AREA.

PROMPTLY SUTEL ADVISING INVESTIGATIVE ACTION YOU ARE TAKING IN THIS MATTER. IDENTIFY THOSE SOURCES AND INFORMANTS BEING TARGETED. SUTEL PERTINENT DEVELOPMENTS AS RECEIVED TO KEEP BUREAU FULLY AND CURRENTLY ADVISED.

INITIATE SEPARATE INVESTIGATION ON THE BLACK REVOLUTIONARY ARMY. IDENTIFY THE ORGANIZATION'S HEADQUARTERS, LEADERS, ESTIMATED MEMBERSHIP, AIMS AND OBJECTIVES, SOURCES OF FUNDS, AND OTHER DATA OF PERTINENCE. SUBMIT RESULTS OF INVESTIGATION ITS REGARD IN FORM SUITABLE FOR DISSEMINATION AT AN EARLY DATE.

END

PLS RPT PAGE ONE THERES AN OVER LINE

PAC FBI NEW YORK

16. Memorandum from J. Edgar Hoover, Director, FBI, to Officers Tolson, Sullivan, Bishop, Brennan, Gale, Rosen, Casper

May 26, 1971

I asked Mr. Pender if he could send down tonight a teletype of just what we have done for the police in these two cases, such as identifying the Black Panthers even though they were not the ones they were looking for. Mr. Pender said they were ruled out. I told Mr. Pender to send a teletype down tonight indicating what we have done and the fact that he attended these two funerals and met the Commissioner and other high ranking officials and offered all the facilities of the Bureau to them because in the meeting this afternoon with the President, and the Attorney General and Mr. John Ehrlichman, one of the principal assistants at the White House, were there and myself, they had the news reels come in and take pictures and the press relations give a statement of what the meeting was for and that steps would be taken to be of even greater help to local authorities.

I told Mr. Pender I would like to have the teletype tomorrow morning in such form that I might send it to the White House so the President can read it. Mr. Pender said that at the funeral yesterday he was notified of a meeting to be held last night and we sent a Panther expert to brief the police department and they went over the case and determined what they are trying to do. Mr. Pender also said that we have notified all of our informants. I told him to include that in the teletype because that is the kind of thing the President liked to know about and told him to give it to me tonight.

Very truly yours,
John Edgar Hoover
Director

17. Letter from J. Edgar Hoover, Director, FBI to Unidentified Party or Parties

May 27, 1971

I have been in touch with Chief of Police John R. Shryock, Kettering, Ohio, President of the International Association of Chiefs of Police, and Mr. Michael N. Canlis, Sheriff, Stockton, California, President of the National Sheriffs' Association, by telephone and have asked them to stand by and be available together with the other officers of each of these associations to be in Washington either Wednesday or Thursday of next week for a very high level conference. I indicated to them that this was to be treated strictly confidentially and did not advise them that the President would preside for fear that there might be some premature leak.

I have also given orders for bringing into Washington 100 of the outstanding police officers of the various communities of the country on June 7th for a two-or-three day training conference to be directed solely to measures to be taken to prevent further assaults upon and killing of police officers. This meeting will be in one of the classrooms of the FBI in the Department of Justice Building and as I understood yesterday, the President had indicated he would like to appear at this meeting and make a statement to the assembled officers. As soon as I have firmed up the list of the individuals who will be here next Wednesday to meet with the President at the White House and the list of the officers of the various police agencies in the country who will be here on June 7th for a two-or-three day training conference, I will advise you of their identities.

As regards the New York situation, following the conference with the President yesterday, I was in touch with the Special Agent in Charge of our New York City Office and, in substance, he gave the following report.

He stated that on the evening of Friday, May 21, 1971, following the shooting of two police officers who were exiting from an apartment house of the upper west side of Manhattan, by unknown assailants, the FBI New York Office immediately established liaison with the New York City Police Department. The FBI's National Criminal Information Center, Identification Division, and Laboratory facilities were made available to the New York City Police Department as well as the immediate and priority coverage of all out-of-state leads by all officers of the FBI.

JEH:EDM (8)

18. Memorandum from Special Agent Ronald Mahaffey to Unspecified Special Agent in Charge

TO: SAC (80-1560)   DATE: 5/21/71
FROM: SA. RONALD E. MAHAFFEY #221
SUBJECT: UNSUBS (2); Shooting of NYC Police Officers
                 THOMAS CURRY and NICHOLAS BINETTI,
                 5/19/71   POLICE COOPERATION

At approximately 9:00 p.m., 5/19/71, captioned patrolmen of the 24th Precinct, NYCPD, were on duty outside the residence of District Attorney FRANK HOGAN at 404 Riverside Drive, NYC. Patrolmen observed a vehicle, occupied by two Negro males, commit a traffic violation (of an unknown nature) and followed in pursuit. Subject vehicle travelled north to intersection of West 114th Street and Riverside Drive, executed a U-turn, and continued in a southerly direction on Riverside Drive. Pursuit continued to intersection of West 106th Street and Riverside Drive, where subject vehicle overtaken by patrolmen and forced to side of road. Before Patrolmen CURRY and BINETTI could leave their vehicle, one Unsub fired a burst from a .45 caliber automatic weapon, critically wounding both officers. Unsubs then left scene, continuing south on Riverside Drive.

Subject vehicle described as a late model Maverick or Mustang (square-backed sedan), black or dark blue in color, bearing possible combination of the following NY license:

8773 YA	8777 XA
8773 XA	8777 AX
8773 AX	8373 YD
8777 YA	8373 YR

Description of Unsubs not available.

All agents are to immediately contact all CIs, PCIs and other logical sources for any pertinent information regarding this matter.

All positive information should be immediately reported to SA RONALD E. MAHAFFEY, Section 221.

1 - Each Agent assigned to the NYO.
    92REM:crp

A Note on the Contributors

(As of Summer, 1993)

The reversal of **Dhoruba Bin Wahad's** conviction is being appealed by the Manhattan District Attorney's office. The outcome could result in his re-imprisonment.

Mumia Abu-Jamal's lawyers are racing to prepare a new legal challenge to his conviction in order to prevent his execution.

Assata Shakur remains in exile in Cuba, where she has lived since her liberation on November 2, 1979 from the state prison for women in Clinton, New Jersey.

For more information please contact:

Campaign to Free Black Political Prisoners and P.O.W.s in the U.S.

Kingsbridge Station — P.O. Box 339
Bronx, New York 10463-0339

Telephone: (718) 624-0800

Initiators
Dhoruba Bin Wahad
Tanaquil Jones